THE WALL
AND
THE WORD

Lessons from the Book of Nehemiah

THE WALL
AND
THE WORD

Lessons from the Book of Nehemiah

PAUL LUCKRAFT

malcolm down

PUBLISHING

First published 2023 by Malcolm Down Publishing Ltd

www.malcolmdown.co.uk

27 26 25 24 23   7 6 5 4 3 2 1

British Library Cataloguing in Publication Data
A catalogue record for this book is available from the British Library.

ISBN: 978-1-915046-54-3

Cover design by Esther Kotecha

Art direction by Sarah Grace

Printed in the UK

'Paul has made Nehemiah come alive in this book. Read it to learn from one of the most inspiring leaders in the Bible . . . a great reminder of the importance of being grounded in prayer and scripture.'

Mari McLoughlin
Church Leader

'Paul's analysis of Nehemiah is rich, incisive and immensely revealing. Every sentence is worth underlining.'

Revd Ian Farley
Rector, St John's Buckhurst Hill

'Paul has been a valued teacher within the Foundations Bible School over many years. His series on Nehemiah was particularly instructive.'

Steve Maltz
Author, 'Jesus Life and Times'

Contents

Part Two: Topics from the Book of Nehemiah

Acknowledgements

This book began life as a series of recorded talks which I presented to my church in 2022. During this period we focused on the book of Nehemiah in our Sunday sermons and midweek homegroups. We were also encouraged to read Nehemiah in our individual devotions. By concentrating on this part of scripture we fully expected to hear from the Lord about how to rebuild our 'wall' and produce a stronger community of believers for his glory.

To this end, I developed the idea of 'bitesize' talks, around fifteen minutes each, the time it might take to drink a cup of coffee. People were encouraged to take a break, put the kettle on and settle down with a hot cuppa while listening to one (or more) of these talks. These 'coffee-cup talks', as they became known, were also intended to help preachers prepare their sermons and to stimulate discussion within the homegroups. In rewriting these talks to form the chapters of this book I have largely kept to the original style, which I hope provides an 'easy listening' approach rather than something more formal.

I am extremely grateful to all at my own church who gave me regular encouragement and support during the making of the original talks. Your feedback has been invaluable.

Thanks also to those who gave me opportunities to teach this material in various gatherings, either online or in person. I am particularly grateful to those who attended my sessions at the Foundations Bible School whose input helped to shape my thinking on Nehemiah.

I am indebted to all at Malcolm Down Publishing for guiding me through the process of producing my first book. Special thanks to my editor, Louise, for her prompt and efficient work, and to Malcolm Down for his clear advice and patience in answering all my questions. Thanks also to the graphic designers for the front cover and the map of Jerusalem's wall, and to Mike Dwight for providing the foreword.

For those who still want to listen to the original talks over a cup of coffee, these can be found on my website www.orchardseeds.com.

Foreword

The impact of Covid in the last few years has been unmistakeable in our nation. Institutions have struggled to survive. Churches, in particular, found it almost too much to adjust and cope with restricted opportunities to meet together. In times like this how do God's people respond? Is it possible to recover and rebuild, and even see revival?

We need answers to these questions, and above all to discover what God is saying to us in his Word. Fortunately, throughout both the Old and the New Testaments, the message comes through loud and clear. It is never too late for God to work. No situation is ever too hopeless. Paul's book speaks right into this in an encouraging and challenging way.

In the Old Testament, Israel repeatedly forgot God, turned away from him, and backslid into idolatry. But God did not give up on his people and he is the same God today. This message came through Isaiah: 'All day long I have held out my hands to an obstinate people' (Isaiah 65:2). And again in Hosea 11:8-9: 'How can I give you up . . . for I am God, and not a man.' It is with this foundation that God understands us, and loves us with a love demonstrated powerfully through his Son Jesus, the Word made flesh, that gives us hope in dark times.

Paul unpacks Nehemiah in a scholarly and practical way. He has a gift for making even difficult truths and passages easy to understand. I have known Paul for many years and I have seen his passion to understand, apply and treasure God's Word in his own life, and then transfer this into others. As a church, we believed the book of Nehemiah to be strategic and life-transforming not only for us but for all churches and ministries at this very testing time.

Nehemiah is a deeply challenging book no matter who we are. It is not all comfortable reading. Every step forward with God will be contested, as is clear in the opposition Nehemiah faced. This testing will be at a personal and corporate church level.

Paul's writing will challenge all of us in positions of leadership. What leadership qualities are needed for such a time as now? Nehemiah's godly humility, strength and courage as a leader, becomes the key to repentance, recovery, restoration, refreshing and revival among God's people. But, as Paul brings out so clearly, what is needed above all is a leadership that inspires and ignites all the people to be involved and be united in seeing the work of God completed. Then we can cry out together, 'Father, may your kingdom come and your will be done in my life and our life together as your church.'

Mike Dwight
Pastor, Missionary and Author of 'Unbeliever to Overcomer'

Introduction

Conversations with My Bible

This book has emerged from what I call 'Conversations with my Bible', time spent talking through with God what he is saying to us in a particular portion of his Word. The result is not a traditional commentary, though in Part One we do cover the text of Nehemiah in some detail and the approach is approximately chapter by chapter.

Nor has the aim been to provide a series of academic studies, though we have not shied away from engaging with some of the deeper issues which come from reading Nehemiah. There were also three topics in particular which seemed to deserve further attention.

Firstly, Nehemiah faced a lot of opposition from many enemies. Why was this, and what could we learn from his experiences? Then there was the Book of the Law, which features strongly in the second half of Nehemiah. What exactly was this? Does this have any meaning for us today? Finally, there is a mention of the Feast of Tabernacles as a notable part of their restoration as a community. Perhaps some further explanation of this feast and its significance would be useful.

It was felt that these topics would benefit from extra teaching, but in order not to interrupt the flow of the narrative in Nehemiah, these topics were picked up after the main series of talks on Nehemiah and each one was put into a separate, shorter series of its own. Here, in this book, these form Part Two.

I mentioned earlier about having 'conversations with my Bible', a term I prefer to that of 'Bible study', for two reasons. Firstly, the Bible is not *primarily* a book to be studied, though for a variety of reasons it is studied, and often to good effect. Study may be part of how we tackle the biblical text but essentially the Bible is different from other books and should be approached accordingly. It is a book to engage in conversation with, for it speaks to us from the one who gave it to us, a God who speaks.

Secondly, the written content of this book has gone through a process of several conversations with others whom I am privileged to teach and share the scriptures with. Out of our conversations together has come a greater sense of conversation with the Bible itself.

In the end, my conversations with my Bible may not be exactly the same as your conversations with your Bible. However, it is hoped that by 'listening in', you will be stimulated to do likewise, not just in Nehemiah but in the Bible generally. We are all to be encouraged to engage with the Bible as a living text, the Word of the living God who desires and delights to talk to us in this way. Listening as we read is an important part of getting the message that scripture has for us.

Christians think of the Bible as inspired, often quoting Paul's words to Timothy that 'All Scripture is God-breathed'

(2 Tim. 3:16). Let's think about that a little more at this point. It is correctly said that for Paul the only scriptures would be what we call the Old Testament (including of course Nehemiah) as the New Testament was not yet written or regarded as 'scripture'. There is nothing 'old' or out of date when it comes to the Bible being inspired.

The actual Greek word which Paul uses is 'theopneustos', which is made up of 'theo' (God) and 'pneustos', which relates to 'pneuma' meaning spirit, breath or wind. The whole word could be translated as 'God-blown' but perhaps 'God-breathed' is better!

But what does it mean to say the scriptures are 'God-breathed'? It is a difficult word to define precisely. For a start, it is found only in this one verse in 2 Timothy, nowhere else in the New Testament, in fact nowhere else in the Greek language until after Paul's time. So did he invent it? Perhaps. Interestingly, there are several examples (some say about nineteen in all) of the church fathers in the first 400 years using the word 'theopneustos' to describe their own writings or sermons. This was not out of any sense of self-importance or claims of divinity, rather that they felt something special had happened as they wrote or spoke. In that sense the word gained a more general use, just as we might also use it of ourselves regarding something we have said or written or taken part in. We were inspired! So it doesn't have to be used exclusively of God or the scripture, and, as we shall see, it can refer to our reading of scripture as much as to the writing of it.

But what does it mean to say scripture is God-breathed? It seems to be a metaphor in some way, what we call an anthropomorphism, as God doesn't literally 'breathe'.

Perhaps Paul is thinking of Genesis 2:7 where God breathes into the dust-made body of Adam and animates him, causes him to be a living being, alive in a new way.

So what actually happened to those who wrote scripture, in particular during the time in which they were writing what is now in our Bible? Peter, in his second letter, says how prophets spoke from God as they were carried along (or moved) by the Holy Spirit (2 Pet. 1:20-21), which could also be deduced from the word *'theopneustos'*. But notice that in 2 Timothy Paul does not say the *writers* were 'God-breathed' rather that the *scriptures* (what they wrote) *are* God-breathed. All scripture is God-breathed. And this is where we come in.

The authors were no doubt 'inspired' or 'moved by the Spirit' as they wrote, but God also breathed on the scriptures at that time in such a way that the words themselves could come to life (again) when read later (by you!). God continues to breathe upon his Word. It was not a one-off capture of a piece of inspired brilliance or a heightened experience in the past (though it may have involved that also), rather it is the Word itself which is living and active, and which can come alive in the moment of being read. What God originally breathed in, is now breathed out.

The main point is not to read 'God-breathed' as 'God-dictated'. Inspiration is not the same as dictation, like an automatic piece of writing. C.S. Lewis has commented that the writing of the Bible was ruled over by a divine presence which inspired without dictating; it was God-directed rather than God-recited.

So the text of scripture is God-breathed in two ways, in and out. Both writer and reader experience its inspiration, though not necessarily to the same degree or in the same way. There remains something of a mystery to all this. However, what we are saying here is that scripture isn't just inspired – it is inspiring, even inspirational. And it is this quality which leads to illumination, and which allows confusion to give way to clarity, so that truth may emerge.

Is this your experience of reading scripture? It can be. Maybe not all the time. I don't think that happens to anyone, but we can always expect this.

I hope this is a useful preliminary explanation of a key word and has led to a better understanding of an important concept that isn't always properly appreciated. We are now ready to go through the book of Nehemiah. So let's begin, starting with some basic facts about the book: what it is like and what it contains.

PART ONE

The Book of Nehemiah

Chapter One

Introduction to the Book of Nehemiah

It is usually a good idea to place a biblical book carefully within its historical context. There are two indications in the text of Nehemiah that enable us to date the book fairly accurately. These are in 2:1, where there is a reference to the twentieth year of Artaxerxes, and later, towards the end, where in 13:6 it mentions the thirty-second year of his reign. Artaxerxes was a Persian king who ruled in the fifth century BC so the book of Nehemiah can be approximately dated as 445 to 433 BC. This means it covers a twelve-year span, which is a relatively long period and much will have taken place during this time that we don't read about, so we should bear this in mind when working through the story of Nehemiah. It is easy to read quickly through part of the Bible and not be aware how much time has passed from beginning to end.

These dates also indicate where Nehemiah fits into the overall span of what we call the Old Testament. You will find it roughly in the middle of your Old Testament, just before Esther, Job and the Psalms. But that is not really where it belongs. Instead it comes right at the end of the Old Testament period. The books of our Bible are not arranged chronologically, nor do they follow the order of these same books in the Jewish scriptures. In fact in the Hebrew Bible Nehemiah is probably the last book of all. Furthermore, it is actually joined to Ezra, which precedes it in our Bible. Together they form a single book, Ezra-Nehemiah, and this is also connected with 1 and 2 Chronicles, which also is a single book in the Jewish scriptures. Put together, these four books, or really just two (Ezra-Nehemiah and Chronicles), constitute a significant portion of the Hebrew Bible, bringing it to a conclusion.

Some think Chronicles should be placed at the very end, but when you look at the last few verses of 2 Chronicles and then read straight on into Ezra you notice something very strange. Ezra begins with exactly the same words as 2 Chronicles ends with. In fact, it seems as though 2 Chronicles ends mid-sentence, and that we need Ezra to complete this. Only when we read through to Ezra 1:3 do we realise that 'let him go up' actually means 'up to Jerusalem in Judah'.

What does this tell us? Firstly, that the same writer was probably responsible for both Chronicles and Ezra-Nehemiah. According to Jewish tradition, this writer was Ezra himself who was known to be a scribe and teacher, and more than capable of putting all this together at some time. He would be the chronicler behind 1 and 2 Chronicles, as well as the combined Ezra-Nehemiah.

Secondly, this overlap between Chronicles and Ezra suggests that Nehemiah may well be best placed right at the very end of the Old Testament. In which case, the final words, 'Remember me with favour, my God' (Neh. 13:31) would be a fitting conclusion to the whole Old Testament, more preferable, perhaps, than the end of Malachi with its reference to God striking the land with a curse (Mal. 4:6).

However, this also raises an interesting question. What then comes after Nehemiah? And the answer is, of course, nothing. At least nothing for 400 years until the voice of John the Baptist is heard crying in the wilderness. Here is an intriguing feature of the book of Nehemiah. Why does it end like it does? It seems to conclude with a strange mix of failure and disappointment as well as success and achievement. This requires some explanation which we will attempt later in this book.

And what does this say about the Old Testament narrative as a whole? What are we now waiting for, and why for such a long time? Again, the answers to these will have to be deferred until we have explored the book much further, but they are worth keeping in mind for now.

Another intriguing feature of the book of Nehemiah is that in the Jewish world it was both readily accepted and yet largely ignored. There was never any question that it should be part of the Jewish canon of scripture. Its place was never in dispute. Yet it sits firmly in the section of their scriptures known as the Writings (or Ketuvim), which was regarded as the least important section after the Law (or Torah) and the Prophets (the Nevi'im). Together the Law, the Prophets and the Writings made up the Hebrew scriptures, which was collectively called the Tanak, an acronym formed from the opening letters of Torah, Nevi'im, Ketuvim.

Whereas the complete Torah was read in the synagogue in a weekly cycle over the whole year, and large portions of the prophets were also included in this, Nehemiah, as part of the Writings, would never be considered in this way. And although some books in the Writings were read during the annual feasts, not so Nehemiah. It makes you wonder whether they ever read it, let alone studied it. Perhaps they didn't really know what to do with it. It is therefore not that surprising that Nehemiah is not quoted at all in the New Testament, nor is it ever mentioned by Jesus. Nevertheless, it remained an undisputed part of their Bible (and, therefore, his), and should be so for us too.

Clearly for the Jews it is part of their history, but it is important to realise that they never regarded any of their books as history books in the way that we do. Books that contained their history were read as 'prophetic', meaning that the purpose of such books was to reveal more about God and his ways, rather than their own past. History really was 'His Story'. That's how we should approach it too. Here is a significant part of God's story; God at work among his people.

We have already said that Ezra was the most likely author of the book of Nehemiah, though compiler might be a better way of describing him. Authorship didn't mean the same thing as it does for us today. Those that look into the structure of the book can see different strands. It was put together using personal memoirs and narratives as well as official records and documents. That's why we get so many lists – those boring bits that we'll try to make sense of later on! Notice for now that the list in Nehemiah chapter 7 is the same as that in Ezra chapter 2, and Nehemiah chapter 9 has a parallel in Ezra chapter 10.

Ezra himself had been part of the previous return (around 458 BC). This is called the second return (the first was under Zerubbabel many years earlier). So Ezra was already back in the land by the time Nehemiah arrived (known as the third return), and Ezra's role will be crucial in the second half of the book of Nehemiah. In Nehemiah 6:15 we read that the wall was completed in an amazingly short time, just fifty-two days. An extraordinary feat, defying normal explanation; one they realised could only have been achieved with the help of their God. So there we have it. Job done! Mission accomplished! End of story . . . but it isn't. This is only the middle. We often find in Hebrew writing that there is a central pivotal point, a climax but which isn't the end. We are only halfway through. There is still the best part of twelve years to go and what happens in this time is critical to the book.

Nehemiah is known for the rebuilding of the walls of Jerusalem. That is what most people would say the book is about. That is certainly very significant but it's not all. The story has only just started. Rebuilding the walls was a means to an end, not an end in itself. Ultimately, people are more important than stones, and the people of God need to become living stones, built together in such a way that brings glory to God and a witness of his love and power to the world. God does not want a collection of isolated stones sitting round like broken down rubble. He needs his people to become a dwelling place for his presence, a holy temple, joined together, built on strong foundations, and rising to his glory. For this something else is needed, the Book of the Law of God, which for us means the whole Word of God, and it is this which will feature strongly in the later parts of Nehemiah where the focus is on the reform of the people.

If rebuilding the wall represents safety, security, even salvation, then that in itself is not sufficient. How to live together as the people of God must follow, what we might term sanctification or holiness, or righteous living. This can, in fact usually does, take longer. Walls may be built in a relatively short period of time, if there are enough builders. Building up people takes longer, and can be just as fraught with difficulty and dangers. God's enemies don't give up that easily. In short, the book of Nehemiah is about two things: the Wall and the Word. We need to bear that in mind from the very beginning.

Let's end this chapter by considering what we know about Nehemiah himself. The answer is basically nothing, or at least very little. He had a father (Hakaliah, 1:1) and possibly a brother (Hanani, 1:2, 7:2), unless this just means a fellow Israelite rather than a family member. But there is certainly no mention of a wife or children, no indication of his age, or when or where he died. There is no background given, and he doesn't seem to have had a special divine calling or great spiritual experience such as Isaiah or Jeremiah, for instance. He did have an important job as cupbearer to the king (more on this later). But otherwise he was quite ordinary, like you or me, perhaps.

His name is based upon the Hebrew word for 'comfort', the root being the three consonants n-h-m. The typical –iah ending refers to God (Yahweh), so his full name can mean 'comforted by God' or 'the comfort of God'.

Incidentally, here's a teaser. How many Nehemiahs are there in the book of Nehemiah? The answer is three. One is obviously our main man. The other two are found in 3:16 and 7:7. These are clearly different people. The first has a different father (Azbuk) and is the ruler of a small district somewhere, and the second came back to the land with Zerubbabel in the first return. So be aware that when you come across this name it may not be the Nehemiah of the book.

Nehemiah may have had an ordinary birth and upbringing, yet he played a crucial role within the purposes of God, and his main calling in life is recorded for all time, and is relevant to all time, including our own. Overall he displayed good qualities of leadership, though some of his later actions are questionable and not really repeatable. But he did have a lot to put up with and we can see him grow into a demanding role.

But how did it all begin? Let's look next at the opening of the book of Nehemiah.

Chapter Two

Nehemiah 1:1 to 2:10

(Part 1)

In this chapter we will begin to consider the opening section of the book, which runs from 1:1 to 2:10. One reason for ignoring the usual chapter division (these are often artificial anyway) and putting these verses together, is that they have a common geographical setting. Before Nehemiah travels to Jerusalem, which is the main location for the book, we find him in Susa, which is where he lives and works.

Susa was a remarkable place. Known in Hebrew as Shushan, it was once a magnificent city, famous and very significant. Today there are only ruins which lie next to the modern town of Shush, situated in what is now western Iran, close to the border with Iraq.

Biblically, Susa is best known for the setting of the book of Esther. Esther married the Persian King Xerxes (also known as Ahasuerus) who, we are told in Esther 1:2, at that time reigned from his royal throne in the citadel of Susa. Incidentally, Xerxes was the father of King Artaxerxes who features in the book of Nehemiah, so chronologically Esther comes before Nehemiah even though it is placed after Nehemiah in our Bibles.

Susa is also mentioned in Daniel chapter 8. Although Daniel was in Babylon at the time, he had a vision in which he saw himself in the citadel of Susa, in the Persian province of Elam. What is remarkable here is that, according to the traditional dating of Daniel, this vision occurred long before the Persian Empire had come into existence or Susa was a place of any importance. Originally, Susa was just a small town by a canal, but Darius I, who was the previous king to Xerxes, turned it into a citadel and made it his capital. He built a large fortress palace there which dominated the city.

By Nehemiah's time Susa had become heavily fortified and was probably the military headquarters of the Persian army. Also, by then, Susa had a significant Jewish population as it had become the home of many Jews who had chosen not to return to Jerusalem.

We don't know why Hanani, and the other men mentioned in Nehemiah 1:2, chose to make the long trip from Judah to Susa. Was it specifically to see Nehemiah and talk to him? Even if Hanani was an actual brother, rather than just a fellow Israelite, it still seems an excessively lengthy journey for a family get-together. Whatever the reason for the visit to Susa, Nehemiah clearly wanted to take the opportunity to ask questions and get an update not only on the city of Jerusalem but on the people in the province generally.

At this point it is worth making a comment about the word 'remnant' which we find in Nehemiah 1:2. For us this can be a rather negative word which we apply to something that is left over and no longer needed, like a piece of cloth to be discarded once a garment has been made. This is not the case when 'remnant' refers to the people of God. In fact, the opposite is intended. Though possibly small in number, the remnant are those that remain at the forefront of God's plans. They are totally dedicated to him and are the ones that God can still use to move his purposes forward and reveal himself to the world.

We live in a time of great shaking. God has been shaking the nations for several years, seeking to get our attention and draw us back to himself. We have seen this in many different ways and throughout all levels and institutions of our society, including government, the monarchy and the church. As the mainstream church is more and more conditioned by the surrounding culture, it inevitably becomes increasingly liberal in its theology, lax in its morality and lukewarm in its preaching of the gospel. It becomes more people-pleasing than God-pleasing. To counter this, God seeks a remnant who will stand firm and not be willing to compromise. While many may fall away (which the Bible describes as being apostate, a military metaphor for abandoning your post), the remnant remain close to God and his ways. They continue to honour his Name and stay faithful to his Word.

Returning to Nehemiah chapter 1, we find that Nehemiah learnt from Hanani that the Jews in Jerusalem were in disgrace or reproach. This was signified by the broken-down wall of Jerusalem. By now the wall had been in this state of disrepair for many years. Maybe they had tried to rebuild parts of it from time to time, but without success. Perhaps they had been only half-hearted in their attempts, or eventually become complacent. Whatever the reason, they lacked the security a proper wall would bring, leaving them open to attacks by raiders and looters who could easily knock down anything their inadequate efforts had constructed.

The state of the wall also reflected the relationship of the Israelites with their God. In those days, a people group was closely associated with their deity. Not to have a strong city in which to live and worship gave a message to others living around them that they did not care about their God, or it might even create an impression that their God did not care about them.

Clearly the news Nehemiah received about Jerusalem affected him a great deal. Whatever the details might have been, just the basic facts saddened him deeply. How do we respond to the state of affairs within our nation, or within the church at large? When we see or hear of disgrace and ruin, do we weep, mourn and fast as Nehemiah did?

In 1:4 we read that Nehemiah 'sat down and wept'. This phrase 'sat down' is not just indicating a physical position but a reflection of his feelings. Typically at that time, to demonstrate that you were in mourning you sat on a low stool or even the floor. Mourning stools were part of Jewish tradition and were even provided in public places so you could sit and mourn after bereavement. It was a visual symbol of the depth of your feelings.

Nehemiah did this for days and days, presumably between the times when he was required by the king to attend to him as his cupbearer. He is weeping over the death of his nation and of a city, and not just any city, but God's chosen city of Jerusalem.

We said that Nehemiah's name relates to 'comfort'. Clearly this news has taken Nehemiah out of his usual comfort zone, emotionally. He is now feeling very uncomfortable. Just as the wall of Jerusalem is broken down, so now is Nehemiah. We will repeatedly see throughout the book that Nehemiah is an emotional man, with strong passions and plenty of determination and drive. But before he can even begin to see what to do, or think how to act, he has to enter an intense time of fasting and praying. God needs him to go through this period of mourning first, in preparation for what is to come.

We said that one reason we should consider the longer passage from 1:1 to 2:10 was because of the common geographical setting of Susa. But there is also another reason. In these verses we see Nehemiah come into the presence of two different kings, the King of Heaven (1:4-11) and the King of Persia (2:1-8). Nehemiah is a servant to both of them. As his cupbearer, Nehemiah serves Artaxerxes, but primarily he knows he is a servant of the Lord God of heaven (1:6, 11), and it is to him, not his earthly king, that he must turn first.

In many ways Nehemiah provides us with a model prayer for such a situation. Notice that it starts with a full recognition of God's character and nature, and in particular it acknowledges God as someone who keeps his covenant. This is always at the heart of our relationship with the Almighty. This is our one hope, our only way to him. He is a God of his word, and he will back it up with action.

If the word covenant is strange to you, then do spend more time checking out this important biblical concept. If you are a Christian, your salvation is based upon a covenant, the New Covenant promised first to Israel in Jeremiah 31:31-34, and extended to both Jew and Gentile by the death and resurrection of Jesus Christ. Christianity is not just another religion. It is a covenant-based relationship with the Lord God of heaven, the great and awesome God.

The heart of Nehemiah's prayer is his confession in 1:6-7. Notice that he confesses the sins of all Israelites and includes himself and his father's house, even if he or others in his family were not directly responsible. This is not about apportioning blame or pointing fingers. But notice also that this is a prayer of confession not repentance. You can only repent for yourself, for your sins, not for others or for what has happened long ago that you were not part of. Repentance is about change which only you personally can make for yourself. However, a general confession in which you identify with the larger picture is valid. Expressing sorrow over all sin is justifiable and profitable. Another, longer, prayer of this kind is found in Daniel chapter 9.

A key point of such a prayer is to admit that God was not unfair in what he did. He always punishes for a reason, and a good reason at that. In the case of Israel, their exile and subsequent situation is their fault alone and not God's.

How did Nehemiah know what and how to pray? Firstly, the prayer recorded for us comes after many days of prayer, fasting and mourning. In 1:5 we read, 'Then I said', and this prayer follows. During those previous days Nehemiah will have been listening to God as well as talking to him, finding out what was on his heart.

But secondly, Nehemiah's prayer was informed by God's Word. He knew that disobedience to the commands, decrees and laws that God gave to Moses would have consequences. For instance, in Deuteronomy 28:52 God promises that disobedience would lead to others laying siege to all the cities throughout the land until the high fortified walls in which you trust fall down. This is part of a whole passage that begins in Deuteronomy 28:15 with 'If you do not obey the LORD your God and do not carefully follow all his commands and decrees I [Moses] am giving you today, all these curses will come upon you and overtake you.'

Also of note is Deuteronomy 17:18, in which one of the duties of the king was to make his own copy of the law, which was to stay with him always. He was to read it all the days of his life so that he may learn to revere the Lord his God and follow carefully all the words of this law and these decrees. Only then would he reign for a long time. Did any king of Israel actually do this?

Neglect of the Word of God brings down walls, making us vulnerable to enemy attack. What was true of Israel is also true of us as individual Christians and of the church in general. For us, it is more than just the commands and decrees found in the books of Moses. It is the whole Word of God. But this still includes our Old Testament. Reducing our Bibles by omission or showing disregard for any part of it, substantially weakens our faith and our walk with God.

Church leaders today are often reluctant to teach the whole Bible. They pay no attention to certain parts of it in case it causes offence or difficulty. They don't want to lose their congregation, so they prefer to follow the culture of the day or the spirit of the age, replacing the Word of God with the more popular words of men or new ideas that people desire to hear. For many, this means ignoring that all Scripture is God-breathed and focusing only on the New Testament, instead of seeing how the whole Bible connects together. The impression given is that the God of the Old Testament is no longer relevant or somehow different from the God of the New. The implication is that Israel is no longer important, the Jewish people are not part of God's plans and we should only concentrate on the church now. Such 'replacement theology' causes great damage to individual believers and the church community in general. To remedy this requires confession in preparation for rebuilding and repair.

Nehemiah recognised from the start that the issue wasn't just about broken walls. It also involved the centrality of God's Word to them. This will become increasingly apparent later in the book. Here in chapter 1 is the first hint of this. If we are to be serious about the book of Nehemiah we must start here too.

Nehemiah concludes his prayer in 1:11 by asking God to give him success by granting him favour in the presence of this man. This is the right order. God's favour precedes any success we might have. We should make sure our prayers follow this pattern.

But there is also a slight puzzle in 1:11. In the presence of *this man*? Who he is talking about? He hasn't mentioned any such 'man' as yet. We will pick this up in our next chapter.

Chapter Three

Nehemiah 1:1 to 2:10

(Part 2)

In this chapter we will continue to look at the section of the book which runs from 1:1 to 2:10. We said in the previous chapter that it was sensible to put all these verses together because of their common geographical setting, namely the Persian capital, Susa, which is where Nehemiah originally lived and worked. It is because of what happens in Susa in this opening section that Nehemiah will leave his home and job for Jerusalem, the location of the rest of the book.

We also said that this section shows Nehemiah in the presence of two distinct kings, the King of Heaven and the King of Persia. By reading on past the chapter division, we gain a better appreciation of how Nehemiah related to them both. There is much to learn from the way Nehemiah conducted himself as a servant of each of them and placing these accounts directly after each other adds to the overall picture.

We have already commented on Nehemiah's approach to God in prayer (1:5-11). In particular, how he confessed it was the past wickedness of his people and their neglect of God's Word to them through Moses which had led to God scattering them among the nations. Though many had now returned, the fact that Jerusalem's wall remained broken down suggested to Nehemiah that all was still not right in that respect.

But Nehemiah also recognised the prospect of restoration. Part of God's covenant promise was that if his people returned to him and obeyed his commands then he would gather them from afar and bring them back to the place he had chosen as a dwelling for his Name. This is always God's heart. 'Return to me and I will return to you' is a theme prominently announced by the prophets (see, for instance, Zech. 1:3, Mal. 3:7). God longs to remedy the past. He wants to rebuild broken walls and lives far more than we do. He will always help once we have recognised past failings and rededicated ourselves to him. We can always be his servants again if we will follow his ways.

So Nehemiah knew there was a way back and part of his prayer was to remind God of this. God hadn't forgotten, of course. He doesn't have memory lapses or senior moments! But praying for God to remember his promises is a way of asking him to act upon what he has said he will do. The old wall may currently still be in pieces but with God's help a new one could be built. You can imagine that Nehemiah probably experienced a mounting sense of excitement as he realised this, and that he could be one of the servants of God who would take part in the rebuilding process. His confidence in God was well founded, but there was a slight problem. Nehemiah currently had other duties, an allegiance to another king, one he served in a different way, by bringing him his wine.

This is the man Nehemiah mentions at the end of his prayer (1:11), and into whose presence he must continue to go every day. He cannot just abandon his courtly responsibilities. He must gain permission to leave, and approaching the king on this matter could be precarious. So Nehemiah seeks God's help once more. He prays for God's favour in this matter. And then he waits.

The two months that are mentioned at the start of chapter 1 and of chapter 2 are both part of the Jewish calendar. These months don't coincide exactly with ours today. Kislev is approximately from mid-November to mid-December, and Nisan likewise falls between March and April. This means that four months has passed since Nehemiah began praying. God's timing is always perfect. Nehemiah had to wait for the right opportunity. He could not force matters. Meanwhile God was preparing and strengthening Nehemiah for the role he was to undertake.

The position of cupbearer to a king was an important one. It involved more than simply being a waiter or a butler. Kings in those days employed people to taste their food and wine beforehand to make sure it hadn't been poisoned. Although this was rather unlikely (other methods of assassination were more popular!), those in power were often paranoid that others were out to get them. It was therefore a useful safeguard to recruit a somewhat more dispensable servant to check that mealtime would be a harmless affair.

Consuming small portions of the king's food and wine beforehand did mean there was some risk in being a cupbearer, but this was not great. There was more chance of a premature death by displeasing the king than by being poisoned. So caution in his presence was always a wise move.

Nevertheless, Nehemiah's position did put him close to the throne. In some cases, a cupbearer was more like a modern valet. He may even become something of a personal confidante. The life of a king was not always one of great banquets and lavish entertaining. A cupbearer was also required when the king dined alone, or possibly with the queen beside him, as we see here in Nehemiah 2:6.

Overall, Nehemiah had a secure job. He ate well and was comfortable in his lifestyle. If he performed his duties proficiently and politely he would receive the king's favour. But, as Nehemiah knew, he needed favour from God also for the task ahead of him, and his prayers were about to be answered in a remarkable way.

For several weeks Nehemiah would have made sure that whenever he was called into the king's presence he looked happy to be there. It was dangerous to give any other impression, so he had to keep his sadness to himself. Nehemiah could not suddenly blurt out his predicament to the king or even introduce it into the conversation. The king had to initiate such a dialogue. But one day, perhaps without realising it, Nehemiah let things slip somewhat and his emotions showed through. This was when God began to act on Nehemiah's behalf.

It was unusual for a powerful monarch to pay much attention to their staff let alone show concern for them. But we have seen that Nehemiah held a rather special position before the king, who suddenly noticed that all was not quite right with his cupbearer. He wasn't ill so it must be suffering of a different kind.

When the king asked Nehemiah about this, he was probably taken aback for a moment. Certainly he was afraid and perhaps unsure how to respond. He starts by greeting the king in the normal respectful way, 'May the king live for ever' (2:3), paying due homage to him. What he says next may seem rather bold, even rude – 'Why should my face not look sad?' However, it is unlikely to be discourteous. It's more along the lines of 'there is indeed a good reason which you have been perceptive enough to notice'.

Nehemiah is also careful at this point. He is wise and diplomatic in what he says next. He does not mention Jerusalem by name. Why would the king be interested in this small distant city? Rather, he describes it as 'the city where my ancestors are buried' (2:3). This is the place that is lying in ruins. This would arouse true sympathy in the king. All rulers in the ancient world were fascinated by ancestry and their ancestors' places of burial. To hear that these places were destroyed or desecrated in any way would cause a reaction, perhaps one of sorrow or maybe even one of terror in case the spirit powers of those who were buried there were offended.

Whatever the reason in this case, the king's response is immediate and remarkable: 'What is it you want?' (2:4). We can only wonder what Nehemiah's reaction was to this. Had he heard correctly? Was the king offering him a blank cheque? But clearly here was another sign of God's favour upon Nehemiah.

He quickly sends up a brief prayer, what we sometimes call an 'arrow prayer'. Perhaps it was a quick 'thank you, Lord' or 'Hallelujah!' Perhaps he needed to double check with God what to say next. The point is that after his days of deeper prayer and fasting, a quick prayer at this stage was all that was needed. Generally, those who are persistent in prayer and fasting find it easier to get answers to arrow prayers in situations of sudden need.

Nehemiah had clearly thought ahead already. He knew what he would need for his long journey and the monumental task that would follow. He would need safe passage and an armed escort, not just to guard himself but also the large amount of expensive timber that he would be taking with him. Also required were letters from the king, official documents to allow him to collect wood from the king's own forest, probably picking this up on the way as he crossed the Euphrates. It may be that these forests were in Lebanon and included some of the finest wood available at that time.

It was astonishing that the king granted all this so quickly and easily. Perhaps he was impressed that Nehemiah had thought about it so much and was prepared to go himself. This was a journey of over 1,000 miles and would take two to three months. The king obviously wanted to know when Nehemiah would be coming back, but Nehemiah couldn't say. Basically it was to be an indefinite leave of absence which we now know was to last at least twelve years, though we read later in the book that Nehemiah did return to Susa for a brief period (though it is not clear how long this was) before going back to Jerusalem again (see Neh. 5:14, 13:6).

We read that it pleased the king to send him, but Nehemiah knew that it was his other king who was really sending him. He acknowledged that the King of Persia had only granted his requests because 'the gracious hand of my God was on me' (2:8).

Nehemiah, whose name relates to God's comfort, was comfortable in Susa but he decided to leave, setting off on an uncomfortable journey into an unknown future. At least it was now springtime, perhaps a better time to travel, so the four months of praying and fasting in Susa may have been beneficial in that respect. But it had been mainly a time of spiritual preparation. By identifying with the sufferings and difficulties of the people of God, those who are defeated, sad and discouraged, Nehemiah had already shown great signs of leadership.

He knew why the walls had been broken down, the reason for their exile and why the city had not yet been fully repaired. At the heart of the matter was obedience to God's laws and commands. Nehemiah recognised that ultimately his task would involve more than putting stones together again. It would require putting people back together, with each other and with God. Here was a considerable challenge.

But for now Nehemiah must have set off with a glad heart. So far everything had gone well. It had seemed easy. His prayers had been answered. The King of Persia had responded positively and with favour. Nehemiah had all he needed.

But wait a moment! Our passage ends with a disturbing note. A hint of trouble to come. Who are these two characters, Sanballat and Tobiah? Will they feature regularly in the book? And what will their role be when Nehemiah arrives in Jerusalem?

In a purely literary sense Nehemiah 2:10 provides a pointer to something to come in the rest of the story. It creates a real cliff-hanger. So we'll end our chapter at this point too!

Chapter Four

Nehemiah 2:10-20

In this chapter we will look at the rest of chapter 2, and in particular pick up that little cliff-hanger that concluded our previous passage, that hint of trouble to come which we find in 2:10.

Who are Sanballat and Tobiah? Where do they fit into this story? What has disturbed them so much and what are they going to do about it? Equally important, we need to find out how Nehemiah responds. In dramatic terms we might say, will the hero of our story cope and come out on top? Will he triumph in the end? Will they all live 'happily ever after'? We'll see in due course!

For now, Nehemiah is on his way to Jerusalem, no doubt in a contented frame of mind, unaware of any such problems ahead of him. All has gone well so far and, in addition, it seems his journey was uneventful. It is simply stated in 2:11, 'I went to Jerusalem', which suggests there was nothing too serious to report.

However, it would have been a long and arduous journey lasting at least two months and covering over 1,000 miles, so Nehemiah does the sensible thing when he arrives. He rests for three days. Not only was this pragmatic from a physical point of view, it also gave him time to think and assess the situation now he was 'on site'. When in Susa he had heard reports from others, but this was not enough. It's too easy to make bold assumptions based upon what others have said. Nehemiah understood that he needed to see the state of affairs for himself, especially before talking to others.

It is always wise before starting a large project to take stock and reflect over the decisions needed and the plans to be made. Enthusiasm and enterprise in themselves are not enough. By examining the walls for himself Nehemiah saw what was really needed and the best way to go about repairing them. He was in no rush. He knew from what had happened in Susa that it was all in God's timing anyway. And what difference would three more days make after all this time? So after a suitable period to regain his strength, he set out one day after dark on his so-called 'night ride', maybe on a donkey or on one of the horses that had come with them.

At this point a map is useful to go alongside your Bible reading. There are many good ones on the internet. Simply search for Nehemiah and walls of Jerusalem. Do include his name, though, or you might get a map from a different period. For convenience, one is provided on page 67.

A map will show you that Nehemiah examined just a short part of the southern wall. He started in the west and worked his way anticlockwise to the east. Specific geographical locations are mentioned, in particular certain gates, whose expressive names often reflected their purpose. These gates had been burnt down as part of the destruction of the city and they would need special attention if the city was to flourish again and provide a place of security.

Nehemiah's initial inspection was brief but sufficient. The remaining part of the wall would be in a similar condition. He went alone, discreetly, and found he could only get so far before his mount ran into difficulties due to lack of space. He was forced to return the way he had come but his diagnosis was complete. He now understood the problem well enough to know what the solution was. Whether Nehemiah had previously formed a plan which his investigation confirmed, or whether his assessment led to a new idea, we cannot tell. But clearly he was now ready to talk to others about what needed to be done.

To this end, Nehemiah called together many people from all levels of society. They must have known why Nehemiah had come to Jerusalem, especially when he arrived with a royal escort and a rather large amount of timber, but motivation was necessary. Those living in Jerusalem had become used to broken walls and a lack of gates. There was no impetus to change. Perhaps there had been attempts in the past to rebuild, but it had all come to nothing. The people were disillusioned. Why bother trying again?

Nehemiah had first to convince them that the current state of affairs was not acceptable. Cities were not meant to have broken walls. Something had to be done. It is noticeable that Nehemiah used two of the words that had been in the report he had received while in Susa – trouble and disgrace (Neh. 1:3).

But under God's hand, disgrace can become grace. Once people realise this, they will agree to anything. What persuaded those living in Jerusalem was not Nehemiah's determination or strong leadership but that he had the blessing and authority of the two kings he served which we mentioned earlier – the King of Heaven and the King of Persia. The response of the people to this was, let's get going then! And so began what is described in 2:18 as a good work.

But (and there's often a 'but' when things seem to be going so well!) that hint of opposition we found in 2:10 comes to the fore again. Now there are three people involved. Geshem the Arab (or Arabian) joins Sanballat and Tobiah. Their animosity and the plans they developed to disrupt Nehemiah are a key part of the book so we will spend quite a bit of time looking at this. But first we need to learn something about these characters themselves and the positions they held in the land at that time.

Sanballat is described as 'the Horonite' (2:19), which most likely refers to his place of birth. Scholars believe this can be identified as Horonaim, a significant city in the southern part of Moab. We find this city mentioned in Isaiah 15:5 and also in Jeremiah chapter 48. Crucially, this means that Sanballat was a Moabite.

Tobiah is described as an Ammonite, Ammon being another territory east of the Jordan River, whereas Geshem the Arab, or better the Arabian, most likely came from a region south of Judah. It is possible he was the chief of an Arabian tribe who had settled in that area.

The name Sanballat is the Hebrew version of Sīn-uballit, an Akkadian name derived from the Sumerian moon god Sīn. This name may have been quite common as it occurs in documents from that time. It can best be translated as 'Sīn has begotten' or 'may Sīn give him life'. This must not be confused with our English word 'sin', however enticing that idea might be, but it does imply worship of a false deity.

Tobiah, on the other hand, sounds more Jewish, and would mean, ironically, 'pleasing to Yahweh', from the Hebrew 'tov' meaning 'good' combined with the typical ending of 'iah' from the opening syllable of Yahweh.

Sanballat, Tobiah and Geshem all held official positions in some way, either as regional governors or military leaders. Sanballat, for instance, is mentioned in certain papyri as the governor of Samaria, dating him as holding this role some time before the seventeenth year of Darius, which is 408–407 BC. Some commentators think he may have also had a military command in Samaria, even suggesting that the word 'Sanballat' is a military title rather than a personal name. Certainly we find him in the presence of the army of Samaria in Nehemiah 4:2, though that could just as likely be in his role of governor.

We may not be totally clear on the exact status of these three, but they would certainly have been appointed to these positions by Artaxerxes and were therefore in the service of the King of Persia. This helps explain the accusation against Nehemiah in 2:19, 'Are you rebelling against the king?' This was a justifiable question, one intended to challenge Nehemiah's authority among the Jews and put him in a difficult situation generally. Presumably Nehemiah had kept those letters from the king which he had asked for before setting out, so his defence in this case was sound. However, although it may have stalled their opposition for a while, they weren't going to give up that easily. In fact, this initial antagonism was quite gentle in comparison with some of the hostility still to come. But before we look at these later attacks upon Nehemiah and the Jewish people there is another intriguing statement by Nehemiah which requires some clarification.

In 2:20 Nehemiah combats their ridicule by affirming his confidence in the God of heaven who will ensure that their efforts in rebuilding the walls will be successful despite any attempt by their enemies to prevent this. Then, regarding these enemies, he adds, 'as for you, you have no share in Jerusalem or any claim or historic right to it'.

This may seem less than diplomatic and more likely to stir up more trouble than diffuse the situation. But is it true? And why would Nehemiah say such a thing? Nehemiah knew the history of his people and the Word of God to them. We need to remind ourselves of this if we are to understand why Nehemiah answered back in this way.

We have already seen that Sanballat was a Moabite and Tobiah was an Ammonite. The Moabites and Ammonites were old adversaries of the Jewish people and we find references to them throughout the early history of Israel. But who were they and where did they come from?

Both the Moabites and the Ammonites were a Semitic people closely related to the Israelites but, despite that relationship, they were more enemies than friends. They owed their origin to Lot, the nephew of Abraham, and a rather distasteful incident.

After Abraham and Lot separated, Lot settled in the city of Sodom. When God destroyed Sodom and Gomorrah because of their wickedness, Lot and his daughters fled to the hill country at the southern end of the Dead Sea. Probably thinking they were the only people left on the earth, Lot's daughters got their father drunk and had incestuous relations with him to produce children. The older daughter had a son named Moab, meaning 'from the father', and the younger gave birth to Ben-Ammi, which means 'son of my people' (see Gen. 19:30-38). The Ammonites were the descendants of Ben-Ammi and became a nomadic people who occupied a territory to the east of the Jordan River. The Moabites also gradually spread over this region, eventually being confined to territory to the south of the Arnon valley (Num. 21:26–30).

In the time of Moses, these fertile plains of the Jordan valley were inhabited by the Amorites, the Ammonites and the Moabites. When Israel left Egypt, their travels towards the Promised Land took them through this territory. However, the Ammonites and the Moabites refused to assist them when they were in need of food and water, even though they were relatives, albeit in a rather unsavoury way. This displeased God and so he told the Israelites to likewise refuse them entry into the assembly of the Lord, meaning that in future they would not be able to join the community of Israel (Deut. 23:3-4). Nehemiah understood this and hence his declaration in 2:20 that even now the Moabites and Ammonites could have no share in the rebuilt Jerusalem. History determined they had no rights in this regard.

Perhaps, then, it was something of a taunt by Nehemiah, reminding them of their past, but it was at least based upon historical reality. It should also be added that when the Israelites were about to enter the Promised Land, God instructed them not to attack, or harass in any way, either the Ammonites or the Moabites, as he had given them, as descendants of Lot, land of their own on that side of the Jordan (Deut. 2:9, 18-19). Israel was no threat to them. God intended peaceful relations between these kinsfolk even if a close family bond was not possible.

But matters hadn't ended there. With a large number of Israelites camped on their border, the Moabites had become alarmed, and their king, Balak, sought aid from the Midianites. As a result the Moabites approached Balaam, a Midianite soothsayer who practised divination. They offered him money to put a curse upon the Israelites. God intervened in dramatic fashion so no harm came to them but clearly this would have created even more bad blood between them and the Moabites (see Numbers chapters 22–24).

Another ploy used by the Moabites at that time was to encourage their women to entice Israelite men. This worked for a while and led to sexual immorality and then idolatry. Once they had become trapped in a sexual liaison with these women, the Israelites were then invited to sacrifice to their gods, especially Baal of Peor (see Numbers chapter 25). One seduction led to another. This, no doubt, was the ultimate aim of the Moabites. If they could entice the Israelites to worship false gods and abandon their own God, then they knew this would weaken the Israelites and maybe even destroy them.

We read in Deuteronomy how God commanded the Israelites not to marry into pagan nations around them because intermarriage would lead the Israelites to worship false gods (Deut. 7:3-4). Such forbidden marriages would particularly apply to the Ammonites and Moabites for this and other reasons (see again Deut. 23:2-6).

From all this we can see why Nehemiah would be wary of Sanballat and Tobiah, and not surprised by their opposition. Ancient hostilities were being renewed as once more enemies of the Jewish people feared what might happen if Israel grew strong again. For Sanballat and Tobiah, suppressing the Jews was crucial. Their personal ambitions required the status quo to continue. They were delighted that Jerusalem's wall was in ruins and they wanted to keep it that way. So naturally they were disturbed, even angry, that someone had come to promote the welfare of Jerusalem and its inhabitants. From the moment of Nehemiah's arrival, even perhaps from the first hint that he was on his way, opposition was inevitable.

And that opposition would build and build. It wasn't just the walls that would be rebuilt, so would this ancient hostility. As the walls got higher and stronger, the level of antagonism grew. We will consider this in our next chapter.

Chapter Five

Further Opposition: Nehemiah 4:1-23, 6:1-14

In this chapter we will continue to look at the growing opposition and hostility that Nehemiah and the Jewish people encountered while rebuilding the wall of Jerusalem. To this end we will jump ahead in the narrative to chapters 4 and 6, coming back to chapters 3 and 5 afterwards.

Something to note before we look into the text itself is where chapter 4 actually begins. Some Bibles (though not many) differ from the standard versions in that the first six verses of chapter 4 are attached to the end of chapter 3, creating extra verses, 33 to 38. Chapter 4 then begins with what is normally verse 7. Chapter divisions are often artificial and arbitrary but it is more unusual to have such an alternative as this. Perhaps this is due to variations in the original Hebrew text. However, despite this change in numbering, the text is exactly the same, so we will keep to the conventional arrangement as it suits better our theme of opposition.

So far Nehemiah had been subject to constant scorn and ridicule, plus accusations of rebellion, all this from Sanballat and Tobiah, contemporary representatives of ancient enemies, the Moabites and Ammonites respectively. And all this before the work of rebuilding had even begun! But Nehemiah knew this work was of God. He had a clear vision and had experienced sufficient of God's gracious hand not to feel overwhelmed. He remained confident of success. However, once the rebuilding started the level of animosity increased.

If Sanballat was disturbed when Nehemiah announced his intention of rebuilding the wall, he was incensed when the work actually got going (4:1). 'Incensed' is already quite a strong word, but this could be expressed even more fervently. He was livid, incandescent with rage. His fury knew no limits. As a result he called others together to express his emotions and to increase the level of ridicule.

We may not be entirely sure who his associates are that are mentioned in 4:2 but presumably they are those he could rely upon to pursue his objectives. Notice also that among those he addressed was the army of Samaria which we said in an earlier chapter might be under his command. Clearly Sanballat meant business and was gathering support.

His remark about the Jews being 'feeble' is a contemptuous one. The word 'feeble' can refer to a flower that has withered but it can also be used to cast doubt on someone's manhood, perhaps in this case suggesting that their muscles don't look up to the task of moving lots of heavy stones around.

How burnt the stones actually were is a matter of dispute. It may be true to some extent but usually it would be only those originally near to the gates which would be subject to fire, and even this would not necessarily affect the solidity of the stones or render them useless. Whatever the reality, this was all part of the attempt to discourage the Israelites.

Tobiah joins in with a taunt of his own, suggesting that it won't take much to bring their efforts to the ground again. Even a single fox or jackal climbing to the top of the wall will bring it tumbling down. An attempt at humour that perhaps could in itself be described as feeble! We shall see later how the Israelites proved him wrong!

Nehemiah's response was to turn to God and give the situation over to him (4:4). In what is a very Jewish turn of phrase, he prayed that what they have wished upon the Jewish people should happen to them: 'Turn their insults back on their own heads.' This may seem rather unchristian, but then they were not Christians! Nehemiah realised that in despising the Israelites, their enemies were despising the God of Israel, so he felt justified in calling upon God to take appropriate action. Again, we should remember the historical background to this antagonism which we explained in Chapter Four.

Moreover, praying like this was better than wasting any effort on their enemies. Instead they devoted themselves entirely to working harder at the wall. It says in 4:6 that they worked with all their heart, in other words they really put their mind to it, not easy if an enemy is having a go at you! Their enthusiasm and industry was another commendation for the people as a whole. In this way they soon rebuilt the entire wall to half the required height. It doesn't say how long this part of the task actually took, how much of the fifty-two days in total. Perhaps it was less than half that time given the difficulties still to come, or perhaps the top half was easier to build once the lower portion was in place.

Whatever the length of time, let's pause to take this in. Already this is a staggering effort. The average height of the wall would most likely be 12 metres, so half would be 6 metres, which is roughly three men standing on top of each other. And this was over the entire length of the wall, calculated to be about 2.5 miles, and with an expected average thickness of 2.5m. Overall, a great start!

Moreover, the gaps in the wall were now being closed. But this only enraged Sanballat, Tobiah and their associates even further, and words were about to be replaced by actions. They now plotted to kill the Jews wherever they found them, which was no idle threat. They had the power to do this.

In 4:12 we find another Hebraic idiom. 'Ten times over' may, of course, be a numerical statement, but just as likely it stands for 'many times' or 'very often'. The point being that, just like constant insults, the drip-drip effect of repeated threats can wear people down. And this seems to have happened. The Jews became discouraged. They looked at the remaining rubble and suddenly thought this is all too much (4:10). Now worn down mentally, emotionally and psychologically, their physical strength started to give way, resulting in panic and despondency. A real mid-term crisis!

Once again Nehemiah's leadership came to the fore. He had practical solutions to the latest threats but the primary need was to refocus the people on God. 'Don't be afraid of them. Remember the Lord, who is great and awesome,' was his rallying call (4:14). 'Remember' is one of the key words of the book and Nehemiah used it again here to great effect. He also declared that 'Our God will fight for us!' (4:20).

But Nehemiah also took sensible precautions from that point on until the work was finished. He set up guards at the weakest places in the wall, armed and prepared to resist any attack, while the others continued to build the wall higher and higher. There was also a watchman with a trumpet ready to sound the alarm if an attack came.

But it never did. The strategy of half the people building the wall while the other half kept them safe, proved to be a sound one, which frustrated their enemies. They knew that God was helping the Jews who, under Nehemiah's scheme, could continue to build from dawn to dark, basically for the twelve hours that constituted a standard day for them. Incidentally, the phrase about the stars appearing was a Jewish way of defining the beginning of night for the purposes of purification or reciting the evening Shema.

The details of the final verse of chapter 4 (v. 23) are rather uncertain. Does it mean they never changed their clothes? Does the mention of water refer to drinking or washing? However, the basic meaning is clear. From this point no-one was ever off duty, with their weapon always at hand. Moreover, for safety's sake everyone stayed in Jerusalem overnight, even if they lived elsewhere.

Eventually the wall was fully rebuilt. No gap remained though the doors were not yet in place; the woodwork was still to be done. This meant that Jerusalem, though easier to defend, was still vulnerable. There is no point in strong continuous walls if the enemy can just walk in through the gates!

At this point, Sanballat, Tobiah and Geshem focused their attack on Nehemiah himself, in what seems more like revenge now the job was nearly done. In chapter 6, they used various ploys in their attempt to harm Nehemiah (v. 2), him with fake reports (vv. 3-9) and intimidate him with false prophets (vv. 10-14) as well as with letters to the influential nobles of Judah (vv. 17-19).

The first plot involved a message from Sanballat and Geshem, whose aim was to draw Nehemiah away from his home territory where he could be attacked more easily. They asked Nehemiah to meet them in a village on the plain of Ono which is nearly 30 miles north-west of Jerusalem. If nothing else it would have been a colossal waste of his time and distract him from his real task. We are not told the reason they gave to Nehemiah for such a meeting, but he spotted the trick and replied, 'O no'! Basically, 'You don't get me that easily.'

Sanballat was nothing if not persistent. After four such failed attempts he adapted his method slightly. It was the same message of invitation but this time in an unsealed letter which was most unusual in the ancient world. Usually a letter had a wax seal to prevent others reading it whilst in transit. This was an open letter, presumably because Sanballat wanted its contents to become more widely known. The messenger, for example, would know exactly what it said and so could easily spread some gossip as he went along.

The contents of the letter were quite alarming. All this wall building was just a preliminary step towards a Jewish revolt and the proclamation of Jerusalem's independence under a new king, Nehemiah himself. His enemies claimed to have proof of these plans, which included the prior appointment of prophets in readiness to declare Nehemiah's kingship. Sanballat's assertion was that the rebuilding of the wall was not merely a defensive measure, but once the Jews felt secure again this would lead to a plot against Artaxerxes and the coronation of the ambitious Nehemiah.

This letter must have really stung Nehemiah. Here was an attempt to destroy his reputation among both his own people and others in the land. Above all, it could create a fear among the Jews of retribution by Artaxerxes. Even the slightest rumour of this kind could be enough for him to send an army to crush such a supposed rebellion.

Nehemiah's reply is masterful. It is direct and to the point. This is fake news! Pure fantasy! What you say is all in your own head, not mine (6:8). Notice that Nehemiah attacks the message and its lies head on, but without attacking those behind it. Instead, his main priority is for his own people. They must not be frightened off from finishing the work. They must not think that completing the wall would give credence to this rumour. They might decide to leave the wall as it was, at half the usual height, so such lies would be easier to dismiss. Nehemiah knows this must not happen. They must press on to the very end.

Nehemiah, as always, turns to God. He prays for personal strength in the face of this attack on him in another of those short 'arrow' prayers that come out of a dedicated and persistent life of prayer (6:9). But no doubt some damage was done. There's no smoke without fire, some might say. Certainly, it is always harder to dispel hearsay and lies once a seed has been sown.

The next attack on Nehemiah seems to follow fairly quickly, giving him no respite. If one ruse fails, just move on to another. Now the source of the attack involved false prophets for hire. In 6:10, one such prophet, Shemaiah, seems to be self-isolating at home for some reason. Nehemiah paid him a visit and receives a disturbing message.

Who exactly is this Shemaiah? There is nothing specifically to identify him except his parental line. Moreover, it was a very common name (there are around twenty in the Old Testament) and he was not the only one to be a false prophet (see Jeremiah chapter 29 for another). The name itself is interesting in that it is based upon 'Shema' meaning 'hear' (as in Deut. 6:4, which contains the famous Shema, 'Hear, O Israel'). As we know, the ending of 'iah' relates to Yahweh, so in full the name means 'the one whom God heard' or 'the one who hears God'. But clearly he didn't hear God. Rather he was paid to perpetrate a hoax.

Here was a man whose spiritual integrity could be bought. He suggested that Nehemiah should flee to the Temple for safety as men were coming to kill him. He offered to meet him there. At night! You won't even be safe in your bed, Nehemiah! The Temple was a recognised place of sanctuary and it was legitimate to flee there if in danger, but Nehemiah knew this was a trap, designed to instil fear, distract him from his main task and make him appear to be a coward.

Again, Nehemiah's response is noteworthy (6:11). 'Should a man like me' means someone in my position. He is not referring to his character or nature, but his role as a leader. Does the man at the top run away like this? Certainly not!

To run away would give the wrong impression entirely and probably mean the wall would be left unfinished.

Nehemiah again showed discernment in the face of these attacks, and there were many of this kind. Several prophets (and one prophetess) attempted to intimidate him and cause him to sin in some way. It is interesting how this is described in 6:13 when it says 'give me a bad name', meaning to discredit him. This is the same expression that Jesus used in Luke 6:22 when he told his disciples they were blessed when men 'reject your name as evil'. This strange phrase in the Gospels is an idiom with the same meaning of giving you a bad name or spreading a false reputation about you. Today we call that slander.

Once again, Nehemiah resorted to a quick prayer, using his favourite word 'remember'. Rather than worry or be afraid or seek revenge, he took the matter to the Lord and asked him to deal with all those who opposed him. He knew that if he kept close to the Lord and continued to dedicate himself to God's work, then their efforts would be futile. And eventually, once the wall was completed, it was their enemies who were afraid and lost all confidence in themselves. It could not be denied that God had helped his people.

However, not all the problems melted away. Tobiah remained a source of irritation and had great nuisance value through his contacts among the Jewish people. We have already seen that he had a Jewish name and now we learn that he had influence through his friends and family in Judah and Jerusalem. We shall see later in Nehemiah chapter 13 how he resurfaced and took advantage of his position to cause more trouble. For now, we find that he continued to send letters of intimidation in an attempt to undermine Nehemiah.

However, with the hand of the Lord upon him, together with his far-sightedness and shrewd policies, Nehemiah was kept safe from his enemies and was able to prosper in his God-given role. Here are lessons for us to learn, and later in this book we will return to how the enemy attacks us, both individually and corporately as the Body of Christ, and what we can do about this.

Chapter Six

Nehemiah Chapter 3

We have just spent time looking at the opposition faced by Nehemiah and the Jewish people. Now, we will go back to chapter 3 and focus on the task of rebuilding the wall of Jerusalem. We will then follow this up in our next chapter with Nehemiah chapter 5. The main reason for putting these two chapters next to each other is one of contrast. Two very different pictures are provided of what life was like within the Jewish community during these weeks of rebuilding.

Nehemiah chapter 3 is all about harmony and a communal spirit, with everybody co-operating as they work together on a common project. In chapter 5 the opposite is to the fore. Here we see internal division, a society split by exploitation and greed. These problems were so real and severe that you could easily wonder if this was the same group of people. How could they have been so successful in building a wall together if there was such discord amongst them?

These chapters also show different aspects of Nehemiah's leadership as the role God had given him starts to unfold. The ability to govern well in all circumstances is an important one to develop.

Nehemiah chapter 3 has been described as a preacher's nightmare, creating an immense challenge to find something meaningful and applicable in its verses. This view is not helped by the comment of one theologian many years ago who offered his opinion that this was probably the most boring chapter in the whole Bible. One wonders whether he had ever read the opening chapters of 1 Chronicles!

To be fair, the chapter is quite tedious as it is largely a historical record of ordinary people doing an ordinary job. But to regard it, as some have, as largely uninspiring with only occasional glimpses of something interesting goes against what we said earlier about all scripture being God-breathed. So let's take up that challenge and seek out those moments of interest and relevance.

Basically, Nehemiah chapter 3 takes us on an anticlockwise tour of the wall as it is being restored, all 2.5 miles of it, enclosing about 250 acres. At this point a map is a very useful aid to go alongside your Bible reading. As we said earlier, there are many good ones on the internet. Simply search for Nehemiah and walls of Jerusalem but do include his name or you might get a map from a different period.

The rebuilding work is largely described in reference to the gates of the wall. The gates were the critical entry and exit points to the city, the places most likely to see an enemy attack. We start in the north at the Sheep Gate, so named as it was the gate where shepherds brought their flocks into Jerusalem. These sheep would be intended primarily for sacrifices in the Temple which was located just inside the Sheep Gate. Notice that the last verse (3:32) brings us

Jerusalem's Wall in Nehemiah's Day

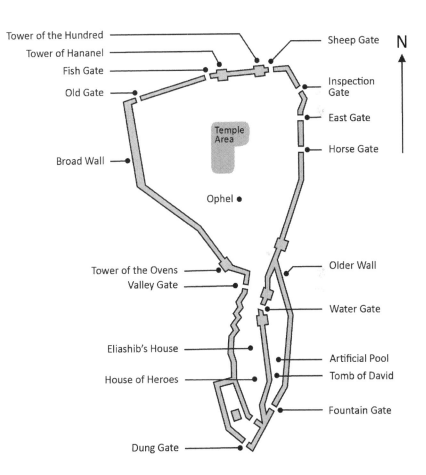

back to the Sheep Gate, indicating that our circular tour is complete.

The first worker mentioned is Eliashib, whose name appropriately means 'God restores'. He was also the high priest, and, together with other priests, he built a short portion before others took over to complete the section up to the Fish Gate. Here was the main 'spiritual' leader prepared to get stuck in and get his hands dirty, which may be why he is listed first, setting a good example. The rest of the chapter contains the names of thirty-eight more individuals and fifteen groups of people. None of these other individuals are mentioned elsewhere in Nehemiah whereas we will meet Eliashib again towards the end of the book.

This section of the wall also included two important towers: the Tower of the Hundred and the Tower of Hananel. The reason for two towers so close together here may be to protect the nearby Temple Mount area, or perhaps it was simply because it was from the north that an attack was most likely to come.

We also read here that this section was dedicated or consecrated, something which is not recorded at this point for the rest of the wall. Was this because it was rebuilt by Eliashib and the priests? Or might it have been the first section to be completed and so worthy of such an event? No reason is given but we do know that later there was a special dedication of the whole wall (see Nehemiah chapter 12).

The next section mentioned is from the Fish Gate (so named because of the nearby fish market) to the Old Gate (or Gate of Jeshanah). One point of note in these verses is the reference to the men of Tekoa. This is just one example among many of people who came from outside Jerusalem to help those who lived there. In several cases, they travelled quite some distance for this purpose. For instance, Tekoa, best known as the place where the prophet Amos lived and worked as a shepherd (Amos 1:1), was 16 km south of Jerusalem.

There is a reference in Nehemiah 3:2 to the men of Jericho, and in 3:13 we come across residents of Zanoah, a place in the western foothills mentioned in Joshua 15:34. In addition, there are many examples of those who ruled over districts or half-districts in various parts of the land, but perhaps most intriguingly of all we read in 3:7 of men from places under the authority of the governor of Trans-Euphrates. You may recall that on his journey to Jerusalem Nehemiah carried letters from Artaxerxes to the governors of this area so they would allow him safe conduct during his travels to Judah (Neh. 2:7). Now we find they are providing workers for the cause.

Also of significance regarding the men of Tekoa is that their leaders didn't, or rather wouldn't, take part. They may have been called nobles but they were far from noble in their character. Perhaps they preferred to stay at home rather than travel some distance to help, but the clue to their attitude is that they wouldn't 'put their shoulders' to the work (3:5). The phrase is literally they wouldn't 'bend their necks', meaning they wouldn't submit. This was the issue. It was not so much about avoiding hard work or joining in with others they regarded as inferior. Rather, it was a matter of submission. Perhaps they didn't like Nehemiah or recognise his leadership. The end of 3:5 suggests this might have been the case. The alternative (footnote) translation of 'under their supervisors' is 'under their lord or the governor', meaning Nehemiah himself. Whatever the correct translation, it seems they weren't used to taking orders and if they couldn't be in charge then they wouldn't be part of this at all.

Did these nobles later regret their decision? We can only hope so. Certainly they have been recorded here for all posterity as the only people who did not join in the work. So well done, Nehemiah, for making sure this was added into the historical document! Of further interest is that later in the chapter (3:27) we read that the men of Tekoa also helped repair another section near the Water Gate. So well done them, for not allowing the bad example of their leaders to deter them from going beyond their call of duty.

Repeatedly throughout this chapter, some thirty-five times in all, we come across the word 'repaired' rather than 'built' or 'rebuilt'. The Hebrew root is *chazaq*, which actually means 'to strengthen or fortify'. It can also be used of people in the sense of encouraging them or making them strong again.

The use of this word might suggest that the wall just needed a bit of repair in places rather than being fully broken down. Perhaps it wasn't such a big job after all. But the Bible is clear how destructive the Babylonians had been (see 2 Kgs 25:8-10, 2 Chron. 36:19), something which is backed up by other historical accounts (see Josephus, *The Antiquities of the Jews*, Book X, Ch VIII). The wall had been completely flattened to its very foundations and needed rebuilding from scratch, though archaeology confirms that the existing rubble was used. New wood was needed but not new stone.

Several times in chapter 3 we are told that those working near a gate also put the doors, bolts and bars in place. However, when considering the opposition of Sanballat, Tobiah and Geshem to Nehemiah in chapter 6, we noted that these were not yet in place. The point is that these chapters are not totally chronological. Chapter 3 contains an overview of the whole work from start to finish with the events mentioned in chapters 4 to 6 occurring at various points during this process.

At times in this list of workers we learn what their usual profession was. For instance in 3:8, among those rebuilding the section from the Old Gate (or Jeshanah) to the Valley Gate was a goldsmith and a perfume-maker, working side by side. How easy it would have been for people like this to try to be excused on the basis they were not professional stone workers or carpenters. We're not trained for this! Give me some gold and I'll lend a hand. Or, I'll just supply some perfume when it's needed. I do a good line in deodorant!

Instead, everyone rallied to the task. It has been said that the most important ability in God's work is avail*ability*. Someone with relatively few gifts or little talent but with plenty of drive and passion can achieve a great deal more than a highly capable person who lacks willingness and application.

Five times in chapter 3 we read of those who worked on the section right in front of their own house. That's a good motivation to do the work well! One such was Meshullam son of Berekiah whose living quarters was, according to the Hebrew word used, simply a chamber, a single small room. Despite his lowly status, he worked just as hard as others to make the whole city more secure.

In 3:11 we find Malkijah son of Harim, who is listed in Ezra 10:31 among those whom Ezra confronted for taking a pagan wife. Now many years later, he was working diligently for the God he had previously displeased.

In 3:20, Baruch son of Zabbai is said to have earnestly or zealously repaired his part of the wall. We may wonder why he is especially singled out or commended in this way. Was this a particularly difficult stretch of the wall? Or was it perhaps because it led up to the front door of the high priest's house?!

We noted earlier that the Nehemiah in 3:16 is not the same as the main character of the book, as evidenced by their different fathers. It is also worth pointing out that the Shemaiah of 3:29 is the son of Shekaniah, a different person from the deceptive Shemaiah son of Delaiah we met in Nehemiah chapter 6.

Another curious feature is a section called the Broad Wall. Archaeology has shown from its remains just how apt its name was, being more than 20 feet or 6 metres wide. Why this portion needed to be so much thicker isn't clear.

The Dung Gate is also aptly named for obvious reasons. Any city needed to have at least one place designated for the disposal of all kinds of rubbish, including animal dung. In the case of Jerusalem this gate led out to the Valley of Hinnom, or Gehenna, to which Jesus made reference in the Gospels as the place of eternal punishment for the ungodly. In the past, this valley was the scene of child sacrifice to the god Molek, and was by Roman times where the bodies of crucified criminals were thrown, which would have happened to Jesus had it not been for the intervention of Joseph of Arimathea.

Just round the corner from the Dung Gate was the Fountain Gate. Getting water into Jerusalem was always a major issue. The only natural source was the Gihon spring just outside the wall at this point. A tunnel had been built by Hezekiah to feed this water into the Pool of Siloam just inside the city wall.

There is only one reference to the length of any part of the wall. In 3:13 it mentions a stretch of 1,000 cubits (500 yards, 450 metres). This allows us to calculate the total length as approximately 2.5 miles. A map indicating who built which part shows some bits were quite small compared to others. But every bit was vital. The wall had to be continuous. Any gap compromised the entire structure. No bit was so small as to be insignificant. Moreover, under Nehemiah's leadership, each man (or group of men) had responsibility for a particular section and this was known to everybody else. This ensured everyone did their best. That part would forever be known under their name and no one wanted to be remembered as a poor worker in God's cause.

Under Nehemiah, goldsmiths, priests and even the perfume-maker became construction workers for a while. They would never forget this part of their life even after they had returned to their usual occupations. Nehemiah had given them all a chance to serve in a different way and they had flourished. This is how to develop people. Get them working together on something and watch them grow. It has been said Jesus didn't train leaders; he trained servants. If we teach people to serve then will see them step up as leaders.

So overall we have seen quite a few points of interest in this supposedly dull chapter. On closer inspection, many fascinating details have emerged. It seems that we can still have a worthwhile conversation with chapters such as these in our Bible.

Chapter Seven

Nehemiah Chapter 5

In this chapter we will follow up our survey of Nehemiah chapter 3 by picking out the main details of chapter 5. As stated last time, there is quite a contrast between these two chapters which provide very different pictures of life within the Jewish community during this time of rebuilding the wall. Gone now is the harmony and communal spirit. Instead we see internal discord and division, a society split by exploitation and greed. Can this really be the same group of people who were working together so successfully?

Moreover, the contrast is not just with Nehemiah chapter 3. Chapter 4 ended on a note of victory as the Jewish people continued to work despite all the external opposition. In total agreement and in full co-operation with Nehemiah's strategy, they armed themselves for self-protection, supporting each other and looking after the needs of everyone. A true brotherhood united against a common enemy.

But now, in chapter 5, everything seems to have changed. For instance, there is no mention of working on the wall. Had this stopped altogether at this point? If so, for how long? Perhaps some work was still going on but certainly it would have been slowed down while they sorted out their internal dispute.

We also need to consider what this chapter tells about Nehemiah's leadership. Overall he comes out of this in a good light, but we could ask why he hadn't seen this problem earlier and dealt with it from the start? It seems he hadn't realised what was going on until it was brought to his attention. In 5:1 we read of a great outcry among the people. Even the wives, a usually silent group, voiced their protest which is only to be expected as this was affecting the children. Which mother wouldn't cry out if her child was starving?

It appears that grain was in short supply due to a famine but it is not clear how or when this started. Famines are usually caused by war or, more likely in this case, drought, though neither is specifically mentioned here. If this famine had already taken hold by the time Nehemiah arrived in Jerusalem, then surely he would have realised something had to be done before beginning a large-scale project like rebuilding the whole wall? This gives rise to speculation that perhaps this wasn't a typical famine but more a problem of distribution. Food was available but was being held back by some in order to exploit others. Certainly the overall impression is of a layered society based upon rich and poor, with the poor getting poorer still.

The king's tax mentioned in 5:4 was not a democratic tax raised to meet the needs of the people. Rather this was a consequence of being subject to a foreign power and was sent to the King of Persia to swell his coffers. As such, the Jewish people had no control over how much had to be paid. What the king demanded had to be given if they wanted to be on peaceful terms with their overlord. As such, it was a punitive tax. Pay up or else!

Moreover, the Jewish people still had to pay the king's tax on their fields and vineyards, even if these didn't produce enough by way of return. Consequently they had to either borrow money or mortgage their lands to other Jews or, in some cases, they had to resort to selling their sons and daughters into what was effectively slave labour simply to keep their family afloat at this time. Overall, for many, hardship was mounting as debt produced more debt, creating opportunities for those who could lend to make more for themselves.

When Nehemiah was eventually made aware of this, his response was initially one of anger. In fact, in 5:6 he was 'very angry', the same strong word that was used of Sanballat when he heard about the wall being rebuilt (Neh. 4:1). Nehemiah's next step was a wise one: he took time to think things through before taking any kind of action.

The Hebrew here is interesting. We read that he pondered about these things. Literally, he consulted himself. It sounds rather amusing, as though he arranged a meeting with himself. Did he draw up an agenda in advance and set a time and place in his diary? Basically, he was counting to ten to let his anger subside so that he could choose his words carefully. He knew he had to get this right. Perhaps he asked himself, 'What's really going on here? What must I do, and when and how?' Deliberate thinking of this kind was better than making rash decisions so he took time out to calm himself down before speaking.

Then he went on the attack, accusing the nobles and leaders of wrongdoing. Nehemiah was no coward when it came to rebuking those in high positions. His anger was a righteous anger and he was prepared to confront them because he knew they were destroying the unity they needed at this point. In particular, he must have been very frustrated that as a people they could stand so strong against an external enemy but fall so quickly to greed and self-interest.

After his own private meeting with himself, Nehemiah then called an economic summit! Or at least a large meeting of all involved in order to spell out what had to be done. One problem was the charging of usury or excessive levels of interest. Nehemiah 5:11 mentions a hundredth part, or 1 per cent, which doesn't sound very much, but commentators believe this was per month, making it 12 per cent per annum, which certainly would be crippling.

The Jewish scriptures contain several statements about usury. One such law is found in Exodus 22:25, 'If you lend money to one of my people among you who is needy, do not treat it like a business deal; charge no interest.' Notice, though, the footnote suggests the alternative, do not charge 'excessive interest'.

Leviticus chapter 25 is also emphatic. 'If any of your fellow Israelites become poor and are unable to support themselves among you, help them as you would a foreigner and stranger, so that they can continue to live among you. Do not take interest or any profit from them' (Lev. 25:35-36). It goes on to add, 'You must not lend them money at interest' (or excessive interest) 'or sell them food at a profit' (Lev. 25:37).

Deuteronomy 23:19 reiterates this, though without the option of 'excessive', when it says: 'Do not charge a fellow

Israelite interest, whether on money or food or anything else that may earn interest.' The next verse says that they may charge a foreigner interest, but again stresses not a fellow Israelite.

Further stern warnings are issued later in the scriptures, for instance Psalm 15:5, Proverbs 28:8 and Ezekiel 18:13. These texts all serve as a reminder that helping those in need should be done without expecting anything in return. Basically, it is wrong to increase your wealth from someone else's misfortune.

The next issue Nehemiah had to deal with involved the selling of their Jewish brethren into slavery. When Judah was conquered, many Jews were sold as slaves to foreigners (Gentiles) and many of them had now been bought back out of slavery by other Jews, as outlined in Nehemiah 5:8. Now some are being sold off again as a money-making scheme. Again, this was contrary to specific laws (see Exodus chapter 21, Leviticus chapter 25) as well as obviously being morally dubious.

Nehemiah didn't mince his words. He did not simply ask the nobles and rulers to think about what they were doing, or feel bad about it, or even just stop it. They had to set things right. Nehemiah did not organise change, he ordered it. He instructed those responsible to put it all right.

Moreover, full restoration was required. If money had been charged unfairly or people treated badly, they had to give everything back immediately, including the interest charged. This is the essence of true repentance, necessary for the restoration of relationship and unity. We read of something similar happening in the Gospels when

Zacchaeus the tax collector responded to the call of Jesus (Luke 19:1-9).

Nehemiah 5:8 reports that the nobles and leaders, when faced with these accusations, could find nothing to say in their defence. Nehemiah had told them the truth and it couldn't be denied. Because he had earlier taken time (with himself!) to think it through, they couldn't argue against his wise words. In fact, to their credit, their response was admirable: 'We will do as you say' (5:12).

Nehemiah had shown good leadership by tackling the problem head on and so had rescued the situation. In addition, he now made another wise decision by insisting they took a public affirmation of their change of heart. By taking an oath in front of the priests, they knew there was no going back. They couldn't claim in future that this was merely an informal agreement which could be rescinded later without consequence. This was now on public record and they would be held fully accountable for their future actions.

As part of this ceremony in front of the whole assembly of Israelites, Nehemiah did something unusual for him. He acted out a prophetic sign by shaking out the folds of his robe (5:13). This is a typical Jewish phrase (literally he 'shook out his lap') which together with its associated action brought the ceremony to a serious conclusion. All that remained to be said was a resounding 'Amen!' from all the people.

The rest of chapter 5 records Nehemiah's personal testimony of how he set a godly example. This may sound a bit like boasting. Aren't I wonderful!? But it was acceptable in their culture for someone in a leadership position to speak in this way about what they did. Moreover, we need to hear this too, to know that he practised what he preached. As governor he could have enjoyed a privileged and luxurious lifestyle. Instead he showed integrity and generosity.

We may not be entirely sure when Nehemiah became governor but this passage suggests it was early on in his time in Jerusalem as it was still the twentieth year of Artaxerxes (Neh. 5:14). It may be that the king had already appointed him as governor and this was explained in the letters Nehemiah carried. Here is your new governor! If so, one wonders what the existing incumbent of the position made of that! Maybe the people appointed him governor soon after he arrived but in favour of the first option there is a hint in Nehemiah 1:8 when Nehemiah makes a request for wood for his own residence, the one he would occupy. As their new governor perhaps?

The point is that previous governors had imposed their own local tax on the people. It was seen as an allowance for the governor and his assistants, who had most likely been appointed to this role by the governor himself. This was a heavy burden consisting of 40 shekels of silver plus food and wine. Nehemiah had the right to demand the same but he did not take advantage of this.

Nevertheless, he did seem to receive a large amount of food on a daily basis, and plenty of wine on occasions, which meant he could engage in some major entertaining. This included not only officials but ordinary Israelites and even foreign guests. There is an unusual reference to poultry in this list of food; unusual, that is, in biblical accounts but historical records do show that there were domesticated chickens and ducks in this region and had been for a long time. Overall, Nehemiah could cater for 150 people at a time. The reference to his table (5:17) is not of course implying he had a large piece of furniture, rather that he had the means of supporting a lot of people in this way.

The overall lesson from this should be obvious. Nehemiah had insisted that others do not take advantage of people, so he must not either. His life must be in line with his leadership. His personal example here is critical. He must demonstrate the same values that he demanded of others. This is perhaps why chapter 5 concludes with this extract from Nehemiah's life, to show the strength of his leadership, and that he never expected more of others than he expected of himself.

The final verse is another of his short prayers, with the now familiar request for God to 'Remember me with favour'. He could pray this because of what he had done for all the people, otherwise it would have been hypocritical.

Above all, Nehemiah has restored unity. Initially, perhaps, he had been too focused on the building project to be fully aware of what was going on in people's lives. Perhaps now he realised that building people into a coherent society was as important as any stone-based enterprise. At least, Nehemiah had now put things right, and the rebuilding of the wall could continue unhindered and at pace once more.

A final point. You may recall that the root meaning of Nehemiah's name is 'comfort'. Here, in this chapter, we see him comfort the afflicted, and afflict the comfortable.

Chapter Eight

Nehemiah Chapter 7

We are now going to consider Nehemiah chapter 7 which, on the face of it, is largely made up of another less-than-interesting list of names (and there's more to come in later chapters). At least here we have some numbers as well (if that helps!). But there is more in this chapter than just a repeat of the genealogical record found also in Ezra chapter 2. The opening few verses tell us about those appointed to key positions in the new city, and the chapter ends with the generous contributions made by those in the past in preparation for future worship and service within the Temple.

We should note at this point the rather awkward, if not strange, chapter division as the final verse of chapter 7 (v. 73) seems to overstay its welcome and tries to begin the next section. So we will leave those final few words of verse 73 for now and pick them up next time as they clearly belong to Nehemiah chapter 8, something which the parallel passage in Ezra chapter 2 confirms.

Meanwhile, Nehemiah chapter 7 begins with a grand proclamation, 'After the wall had been rebuilt', picking up on Nehemiah 6:15 where we are told the wall was completed after fifty-two days. Hallelujah! Job done!

Mission accomplished! And in the face of such great odds. There were so many reasons why this shouldn't have happened at all, let alone in such a remarkably short time. This was a real work of God and must have been a great relief all round.

But this is not the end of the book. In some ways, it's just the beginning. Or at least we have reached a pivotal point. What happens next, now that the wall has been rebuilt? What we find here is a shift in emphasis from the new city to the new society, from stones to people. Previously in Nehemiah the primary focus was the wall. The people were there for the sake of the wall. They served it. Now fully built, the wall is there for the sake of the people. It will serve them.

This was the real purpose all along. After all, people are more important than stones. Now it is time to rebuild them, to focus on the society within the wall. This change in emphasis becomes even more apparent as we go through the second half of Nehemiah, especially once Ezra starts reading the Law. Overall, Nehemiah is a book of two halves: the wall and the Word.

We are told something else important at the start of chapter 7: all the doors are in place. These doors, or really gates, have now also been finished and made secure. And so, to this end, gatekeepers are appointed. The theme of gates and gatekeepers is such a crucial one that more will be said on this later in our book. For now, let's understand that the gatekeepers were the first group to be mentioned as being appointed. This was not an optional extra but something vital to the city. Their job was not like that of a hotel doorman, for instance. It involved far more than just opening and closing. Gatekeepers were more a cross between security guards and maintenance men. They had to keep an eye out for invaders, those whose presence in the city was not welcome, and also keep a check on the state of the gates to see if further repairs were needed. In both these ways we can say that they functioned as watchmen.

Other groups appointed at this time were the singers and the Levites, those who were to lead in worship and those who were to help in teaching. We will see both of these groups in action in later chapters, but for now we simply note that these were teams not just individuals, and with roles that were clearly defined and known to others.

As for who appointed these groups, this isn't explicitly stated. It may have been Nehemiah but whereas in the text he says, 'I had set the doors in place' (v. 1), the rest of the verse merely says these groups were appointed. However, in verse 2 Nehemiah himself does make one significant appointment, or perhaps two. The Hebrew of this verse isn't totally clear. Hanani and Hananiah could be two different people with two different roles, or it could be read as 'Hanani who is also called Hananiah', suggesting that the latter is his full name but he is usually known by the contraction, Hanani. It would also seem that Hanani is the same person that was mentioned in Nehemiah 1:2 as one of those bringing news of the state of Jerusalem to Nehemiah while he was in Susa. There, as also here, he is described as 'my brother' or 'one of my brothers' suggesting he may have been a personal relative rather than just a fellow Israelite.

What is clear is that he was given an important job. He was put in charge of the city! If he is the same person as

Hananiah then he was already commander of the citadel, the fortress in the north of the city, so such a promotion could seem sensible. Evidently, Nehemiah, who presumably remained as governor, was prepared to delegate. Perhaps he wanted to show that he was not in this for personal or political glory, especially after being falsely accused in Sanballat's letter (in Nehemiah chapter 6) of wanting to become king of Jerusalem!

Hanani was well equipped for his enhanced position as he displayed two essential qualities of leadership: integrity and fear of the Lord. His integrity, based upon the word for faithful, meant that he would not be knocked off course by anything; and his fear of the Lord signified that in everything he lived in full awareness of Almighty God and so would be afraid of nothing or no-one else.

In verse 3 we come back to the gates and their significance. Nehemiah gives a clear instruction about when they are to be opened and closed. This verse contains a very Jewish way of expressing time. The gates are not to be opened until the sun is hot. You don't need me to tell you that the sun is always hot! Very hot! Apparently it's around 6,000° Celsius on its surface and 15,000,000° Celsius at its core. And, of course, no-one switches it off at night and on again in the morning. But in those days the time of day was measured not so much by the amount of light but the amount of heat. 'Until the son is hot' means when the sun is at its height and the day is well established. Basically, don't open the gates at daybreak, at first light. Wait until the day is well advanced. And they were to be closed again in good time before the sun went down, which was one of the main responsibilities of the gatekeepers.

In most cities in those days, the length of time in which the gates were open was quite short, and if there was a threat of war or any kind of trouble then the opening hours were significantly decreased. Here, for the rebuilt gates of Jerusalem, this was to be about six hours maximum, from midday to 6pm. There was still a need for high security for this fledgling new city.

As well as the appointed gatekeepers, other residents also had to keep watch. Walls do not guard themselves. Diligent watchmen are needed. Continual vigilance is always necessary otherwise all the hard work of rebuilding can easily be undone. This is an important principle within our Christian lives individually and corporately, so we will return to this again later in this book, in Part Two.

Everything was now in order, both practically (walls, gates, gatekeepers) and spiritually (singers, Levites). The wall had not been rebuilt so that the people of Jerusalem could spend time looking at some well-constructed stonework. Rather, it had been rebuilt so that they could now worship God with greater freedom and security, and learn from the Word of God in peace and safety.

So far, the city was yet to be fully repopulated (we will learn about this later in Nehemiah chapter 11) and much of the housing remained abandoned or in ruins. It is not surprising that Jerusalem had few inhabitants when its wall was in pieces, but now things could be different. A new normal could emerge.

So Nehemiah now had a new task from God, who put it in his heart to recreate the city within the wall, the new society that would truly make it the city of God. To this end he wanted to know exactly who had returned from exile in the first place, many decades earlier under Zerubbabel. So he dug out of the archives the old genealogical record which, as we said earlier, was largely identical to that also recorded in Ezra chapter 2. Don't ask me why some of the names or numbers don't quite match, or why the verse numbering is slightly different in places! No doubt inaccuracies do occur in historical documents.

Incidentally, in case you're wondering (and you can't be bothered to check!) the numbers in verses 8-62 of Nehemiah chapter 7 don't quite add up to the 42,360 mentioned in verse 66. Their total is slightly less. So it seems some people were counted but not attributed to their family line. Does any census get everything entirely right?

But this slight numerical deficiency was nothing in comparison to the much more serious problem which is mentioned in verse 64. The priestly records were not complete. Some bits had gone missing! These records would have been taken with them into exile in Babylon but apparently not everything had survived the journey. Lost data is not just a modern problem it seems.

But this was a real blow to those concerned. Without their family record they couldn't serve as priests. According to their law it was essential that they could determine their lineage to establish that they were descended from Aaron, the brother of Moses and the first high priest of the Israelites. Without this they were designated as 'unclean', meaning that they were excluded from any priestly duties.

There are two intriguing details in verse 65 that are worth commenting upon. Firstly, there is a reference to the governor. He was the one who enforced this ruling. This wasn't, of course, Nehemiah, who wasn't around at the time of the first return from exile. This was one of his predecessors, which shows that they had governors from the moment they first came back to Jerusalem.

In addition, there is mention in this verse of the Urim and Thummim. In the past these had provided a means of decision making or revelation that was entrusted exclusively to the high priest (see Exod. 28:30, Lev. 8:8). What exactly these two objects were is not known as no description of them is ever given. However, they must have been small and relatively flat as they were stored in the breastpiece of the high priest. This breastpiece was a small pouch forming part of the high priest's ephod, which was a sleeveless garment rather like an apron. The breastpiece itself was inlaid with twelve precious stones and engraved with the names of the twelve tribes of Israel. It was also known as the 'breastpiece of decision' because it housed the Urim and Thummim.

The use of the Urim is found in Numbers 27:21, and the latest evidence of its use is in the time of David. This mention in Nehemiah of the Urim and Thummim is the only such post-exilic reference. Perhaps it was revived here as a temporary measure in order to determine if these people were of the priestly line or not. If so it was presumably seen as a reliable way for God to reveal this important information.

For us, this catalogue of names and numbers may seem rather tedious but in effect this is an important roll of honour. These people were important to God because they did what so few of their fellow Jews had done. Only about 2 per cent of the total number of those carried away into exile actually returned, so they are deemed worthy of being cited in God's Word for all time. They took the trouble to return to the land God had given them after they had already been settled elsewhere for seventy years. They had a pioneer spirit and felt a call from God. Their own priorities were less important even if it meant a certain amount of hardship to uproot and go back. So they are deemed worthy of a double mention, once in Ezra chapter 2 and again in Nehemiah chapter 7.

But what is perhaps rather curious about this, is that the list occurs twice in what is effectively a single book of Ezra-Nehemiah, and especially so if Ezra was the author of both parts. Maybe Nehemiah insisted it was also put in the account of the work he had been overseeing. They are to be reaffirmed as, without them, what he had achieved could not have happened. Although we learn in 7:73 that they mostly settled in their own towns rather than in Jerusalem at that time, they (or at least their families) had now responded to Nehemiah and were the future of the city. They will repopulate it, serve God in it and preserve it for those to come.

This list reminds us that the work was really about people. The wall in itself wasn't all that meaningful. What was of value was the benefit the wall would have in the lives of God's people, enabling them to live, work, worship and study in peace and security.

Everything was now ready for worship and celebration. But first something else was essential. The Book of the Law of God had to be read, and listened to attentively.

We'll turn to this in our next chapter.

Chapter Nine

Nehemiah Chapter 8

We have reached a significant moment both in the narrative of the book of Nehemiah and in the life of the Jewish people at that time. It is now the seventh month, known as Tishrei. Moreover, it is the first day of that month (8:2) so it is only five or six days after the wall was completed which was on the twenty-fifth day of Elul, the sixth month (Neh. 6:15).

At this point we should say something about the Jewish calendar year and, in particular, about one peculiar feature, namely that there are actually two starting points, or New Years. (In fact, in total there are four New Year's Days, but we will ignore those for animals and trees!) The Hebrew calendar is a lunar one, which makes it a bit more complicated than ours. It usually has twelve months of thirty days, but occasionally it has thirteen months. Every so often there is the need to introduce an extra 'leap month' to prevent the feast days slowly moving into the wrong season of the year.

In Exodus 12:2 God instructed the Israelites to regard the month of their liberation from Egypt as the first one of their year. This month is called Nisan and begins their cycle of feasts, starting with Passover in what we call springtime.

This created a religious calendar or spiritual year for them. On this basis, Tishrei is the seventh month occurring in our autumn. In this month they celebrate the Feast of Tabernacles, from the fifteenth day of that month. We will read about this in Nehemiah chapter 8, and because it is important for Christians to understand this feast we shall feature it again later in this book, in Part Two.

But this feast of Tabernacles is also called the Feast of Ingathering, as it occurs at harvest time, and in Exodus 23:16 we read that this is to be celebrated at the *end* of the year. So Tishrei is also seen as a changeover month to a new year, an agricultural year based on farming. Today, the start of Tishrei is the official Jewish New Year (called Rosh Hashanah). It begins the civil year rather than the religious one, which still starts in Nisan.

Which of these New Years came first is an interesting debate. Some say Nisan was the original start of the year, long before it was proclaimed as such to Moses, and that Tishrei was only recognised later. Others say Tishrei naturally came first as it was based upon the agricultural cycle and therefore would pre-date the command in Exodus when God initiated a second New Year to remind them of their new start after being set free from slavery in Egypt. Certainly there is some evidence for this. For instance, some ancient farming calendars from before the time of Moses show the year starting just after the ingathering of crops. To bolster that view, some ancient rabbis state categorically that God created the world in the first week of Tishrei!

Basically, the first of Nisan is the New Year for kings (defining the regnal years) and for festivals, as God himself 'appointed' the festivals, and the first one in the list was Passover. The first of Tishrei was declared to be the New Year 'for the years, for sabbatical years, Jubilee years, and for planting and vegetables'. As farming was originally the main economic activity this date also defined the fiscal or tax year. In the time of Jesus, both New Years were recognised.

If you think this is all rather strange, bear in mind that as well as our standard year from January to December we also have a financial year, starting in April, and a school or academic year, starting in September. And the last two don't even begin on the first day of a month!

Nehemiah chapter 8 is also significant in that Ezra now comes onto the scene and plays a major role in what will happen next. This is the first mention of Ezra in the book of Nehemiah but, of course, he had been there all along, having arrived in Jerusalem about thirteen years before Nehemiah. Presumably he had done his bit in rebuilding the wall, though he is not named in this way.

Ezra had a priestly background. Fortunately, his lineage was not one of those that had gone missing while in exile (see back to Neh. 7:64). It is given in great detail in the opening five verses of Ezra chapter 7, and shows an exemplary pedigree, going back to Aaron via Eleazar, Phinehas and Zadok, among others.

But Ezra was also a scribe and teacher who 'devoted himself to the study and observance of the Law of the LORD, and to teaching its decrees and laws in Israel' (Ezra 7:10). It is generally accepted that it was Ezra who had established Torah-based synagogues for the Jewish people while in exile, and tradition adds that he became the president, or leading figure, of the Council of 120 Jews known as the Men of the Great Assembly (also called the Great Synagogue) which eventually decided which scriptures should be included in the Jewish canon. As we have said before, it is most likely he wrote or at least compiled the final version of Ezra-Nehemiah as well as the Chronicles. Overall, he was the ideal man for the next phase of God's rebuilding plan, which was to build up his people into a God-fearing and Torah-observant community.

To go alongside this impressive CV is his noteworthy name, which derives from the Hebrew word *ezer*, meaning 'a help' or 'helper'. This he was certainly going to be, to Nehemiah, to the Jewish people, and to God. We recall in Nehemiah 6:16 that the work on the wall was only completed in such record time 'with the help of our God'. Now God's help for this new task was going to come in the form of the person of Ezra.

It is worth adding here that Eve was also described as a helper to Adam. The phrase in Genesis 2:18 is *ezer kenegdo*, which more literally means 'a helper suitable' to Adam, one who comes alongside and fits perfectly for the joint task. Also, in the New Testament the Holy Spirit is described as our helper, usually translated Counsellor, as he is the one who comes alongside (in Greek, *parakletos*) in order to strengthen, comfort and teach Christian believers.

There is now a need to draw the people together around the Word of God, and Ezra will be a significant help in this. We might recall that some of the problems found in Nehemiah chapter 5, which we discussed earlier, came from the people no longer obeying what God had previously said in their Law. So it was clear that something had to be done, and it was.

Nehemiah chapter 8 stresses the centrality of the written revelation of God. We should note from the opening verse that it was the people who told Ezra to bring out the Book of the Law of Moses and read it to them. This was something the people wanted. It was not forced upon them. Clearly God's Spirit was at work among them, creating a hunger and desire to hear it, understand it, and obey it. The fact that they assembled as one man also indicates that they were moved by the Spirit to receive what God's Word had to say to them. Would that we would see this more often in our church communities today.

Such a large gathering as this would require a spacious open area, and the square near the Water Gate proved ideal. As for what Ezra brought out and read from, this is described in Nehemiah 8:1 as the Book of the Law of Moses. Later in this chapter it is called the Book of the Law of God (v. 8, 18) and elsewhere as the Book of Moses (Neh. 13:1) or just simply the Law. What exactly was this? All the first five books of the Bible? Just Deuteronomy, as a summary of them? Or something else which we don't have today? We will leave this unanswered for now and pick it up later in our book as the theme of the Law is such a crucial one, and often misunderstood by Christians today who are confused as to what it might mean for them. This deserves fuller treatment, so a section in Part Two will be dedicated to this rather than interrupt our consideration of chapter 8 as a whole.

The group that Ezra addressed included men and women and indeed everyone capable of understanding, which probably means children above a certain age. Usually only men were taught the Law, but here women were also included as everyone needed to hear this. Perhaps the idea was that the women needed to know the Law so they could check up on their menfolk afterwards!

A certain amount of thought and practical consideration had gone into the planning of this event. A wooden platform was built so that Ezra could be seen by everyone and so that his voice would carry over the large crowd. The timing was also carefully arranged. This was not going to be a short affair. Lasting from daybreak (literally, from the light) until noon this was to be a six-hour marathon for everyone involved. But at least it wasn't the hottest part of the day which would make it more bearable, although everyone was standing for that length of time. Incidentally, you will recall from Nehemiah 7:3 that the gates were to be kept locked until midday, so during these six hours there would be no distractions from outside. It also meant no-one could sneak out through the Water Gate for a quick break. A captive audience indeed!

But why would anyone want to slip away given the importance and value of the occasion? To go missing would mean missing out. They had gathered from dawn to hear God's Word, showing a great willingness to make sacrifices for that purpose. And so, we read that they listened attentively (8:3). They also praised God with lifted hands, loud 'Amens', and faces bowed down to the ground in worship. This was a great experience to be part of, not one to avoid.

Ezra had some assistance in this task of getting the Law of God off the page and into people's lives. There were six or seven men standing on either side of him, though it is not totally clear what their function was. In addition a dozen or so named Levites were mingling with the crowds to help them understand what was being read out. It is all very well proclaiming God's Law, and certainly there is value in just hearing it, but it is less meaningful if there is little or no understanding of its actual message or relevance.

Nehemiah 8:8 states that these Levites (or learning assistants as we should perhaps think of them) were there to 'make clear' to the people what they were hearing and where necessary to read bits again and explain its meaning. The footnote alternative to 'make clear' is 'translate', which might suggest that some of the inhabitants of Jerusalem were not yet familiar enough with the written Hebrew language to pick up everything straightaway. But it might simply be that the Levites were on hand to help people translate the words into action, to know how to respond in their lives to what they were hearing.

The point is that understanding needs to be the primary goal of any preacher or teacher. Learning is the real aim, not just speaking, and, let's face it, we can all be a bit slow at times to fully grasp what we hear. Time is needed to check out what has, or has not, been understood. This should not be rushed. It was often said by the rabbis that it took only hours to read the Law but a lifetime to apply it.

Once the people heard the Law and understood it they responded by weeping, showing they had indeed grasped its message and recognised that things were not as they should be. They were showing true repentance. Sometimes it hurts to be reproved and corrected; these tears were evidence of that. But the people were told this sadness was not to last. Once they had grieved over their sins it was time to receive the joy of the Lord and begin to celebrate. It is good to be sad under the conviction of the Holy Spirit through the Word of God, but this eventually must give way to joy once repentance has achieved its aim.

That day, the first day of Tishrei, had been a special one, but it was only a start. The next day the leaders and heads of families met again with Ezra for further instruction. Again, they gave attention to the Law, and it was then that they discovered written in its pages something which had been ignored for a long time. This seventh month contained a special feast, the Feast of Tabernacles or Booths. This was a celebration of how God had provided for Israel in the wilderness and was to be re-enacted at this time of year in remembrance.

Once this was realised, they spread the word not just in Jerusalem but also in surrounding towns. In particular, this seven-day festival was to start on the fifteenth of Tishrei so there was still time to observe it this year. As this involved them living in specially constructed booths during this period, they hurried out to get the necessary branches. Everyone took part. Those that had houses built their booths on the roof; others used whatever suitable space in the city they could find.

Whatever had been read to them by Ezra the previous day, it is now clear they were studying parts of Exodus or Leviticus. It is always good to find new things in God's Word and put them into practice at once. This feast must be revived! Let's do it! And it didn't stop there. On every one of the seven days, and on the extra final eighth day, they continued to read the Law. What else might they find!?

The Feast of Tabernacles is designated as a time of great joy, and this certainly was their experience at this time of its renewal. For many Christians too, this is a forgotten or undiscovered feast which should be better understood, so we will return to this again in Part Two of this book. Meanwhile, we will turn next to Nehemiah chapter 9.

Chapter Ten

Nehemiah Chapter 9

The events of Nehemiah chapter 9 occur just two days after the end of the previous chapter. It is now the twenty-fourth day of the seventh month (Tishrei) and the Feast of Tabernacles has recently come to an end. After this eight-day festival, full of joy and celebration, what happened next?

The answer is perhaps rather surprising. The Israelites continued to gather together but this time for prayer, fasting and confessing their sins. But there is a good reason for this which we discover at the end of the chapter and on into chapter 10. In fact, these two chapters of Nehemiah are linked and really form one single passage.

As part of this special day, the Israelites continued to read the Book of the Law. Now they had started getting back into the Word they weren't going to give it up. On this occasion they read it for a quarter of the day, that's three hours out of the twelve hours of daylight. This was followed by a further three hours of confession and worship. Here was an intense time of refocusing on God, complete with outward signs of what they felt inside. They had changed their usual garments for ones of sackcloth, a more uncomfortable rough fabric than their usual linen tunics. They also had put dust, or small handfuls of dirt, on their heads. These dramatic gestures were a public demonstration that they were troubled by their sin and felt a real poverty of spirit when it came to standing before God.

And stand was what they did for all these hours. There are four references to standing in these opening verses of chapter 9, including the Levites standing on some stairs in verse 4, and the well-known exhortation in verse 5 to 'stand up and praise the LORD your God, who is from everlasting to everlasting'.

It is noticeable that for this period of repentance those of pure Israelite blood separated themselves from those who were considered as foreigners. This was because they were about to confess the sins of their 'fathers', meaning their Israelite ancestors in general, and this was not something non-Israelites could do in any meaningful way. Within Israel (and elsewhere) it was usual to glorify your forefathers, so to confess the sinfulness of those who had gone before you was significant and would add to the seriousness of the occasion.

Something for us to learn from this passage is that repentance or confession isn't something that we do once or twice and then consider to be over and done with. Here we find that the closer they drew to God, the more they sensed the need to repent. This humble gathering of God's people occurred straight after the end of a joyful celebration of his goodness towards them. A new awareness of his presence and a fresh vision of who he was, did not lead to complacency or self-satisfaction. Rather it drove them to seek him more.

By far the bulk of this chapter is a prayer, and a very public one, unlike the similar one in Nehemiah chapter 1 which was Nehemiah's private prayer following his personal time of mourning and fasting. The Old Testament records other prayers that have a similar style and content to those in Nehemiah, such as Daniel's prayer in Babylon shortly before permission was first granted for the Jews to return to Jerusalem (Daniel chapter 9). Another example, and one more recent to Nehemiah, is in the book of Ezra where the scribe's personal confession of the shame and disgrace of his people soon turned into a more public display of weeping by a large number of Israelites who came to the same realisation of what they had done wrong (Ezra chapters 9 and 10).

In Nehemiah chapter 9 it was the Levites who took the lead in this time of prayer, calling out with loud voices to the Lord (9:4). We may not be totally sure how this worked in practice. Did they all pray out loud at the same time? Presumably not, for the sake of clarity. Perhaps it was written out and they took turns in praying certain portions. One Jewish tradition says that Ezra wrote out the prayer beforehand or even prayed it himself and the Levites joined in. Or it may be that this group of Levites spontaneously prayed in succession and what is recorded here is just a summary of their praying, though its format suggests that at least in its final form it had been carefully constructed. Whatever actually took place that day, this may still simply be a brief record encapsulating what was prayed at that time. Although this prayer is thought to be the longest written prayer in the Bible, it still only takes five or six minutes to recite, a useful reminder that prayer does not need to be long to be glorious and effective.

Although the main purpose of the prayer was to confess their repeated rebellion against the Lord, it does not spend all its time in deep introspection. Sinful people need to look outward to God and not just inward to themselves. Once we realise our sin and feel convicted about it, we should turn our eyes away from the problem and towards the solution, Almighty God himself.

In our prayers, a good start is always to refresh our understanding of God as the creator of all things. After all, this is where he began his part in our human story and without this we wouldn't have any life at all. Declaring that God made all things sets him apart, and does wondrous things in our spirit, the very depth of our being. 'You alone are the LORD' (9:6). And not only did he create all that we can see and experience, but he is also the maker of the highest heaven, which means the invisible or spiritual world currently beyond what we are familiar with.

Stand up and praise the Lord your God, who is from everlasting to everlasting. He has no beginning or end. Here is a tremendous reason to humble ourselves and exalt him. Another is that the multitudes of the heavenly hosts worship him, constantly (9:6).

However, this is not only a God who has created but one who continues to help, guide, redeem. He is involved in all aspects of life, being both transcendent (well beyond anything we can imagine) and immanent (so close we can feel his presence at times). And so in this prayer there follows a review of what God has done for them, his people. We find something similar in Daniel's prayer in Daniel chapter 9 and in Stephen's testimony before the Sanhedrin in Acts chapter 7 as well as in some of the psalms.

However, this is not so much a matter of recounting their history (Jews at the time didn't think that way) but of retelling the story of God and his dealings with them. This had started with God choosing an individual, Abraham, and making a covenant with him and his descendants. It is only because God had promised this land to Abraham that they are there now. God's promises are true, and he keeps them, always.

And so, through Abraham, began their journey into an understanding of this God of all the universe, who is their God but much more too. They had got to know God through his mighty works on their behalf. That is always the case. Through the works of God, we come to know the ways of God, and then we can understand the will of God.

In 9:10 there is a wonderful phrase. Following God's mighty works in rescuing his people from slavery in Egypt, it says, 'You made a name for yourself, which remains to this day.' What an extraordinary but very meaningful statement. One version has that God had 'won himself a name'. Basically it means that through this event he had gained a reputation, and in particular he was now more widely known, not only among the Israelites or indeed the Egyptians but among all nations as news of this great exodus spread throughout the known world. We see an example of this when Rahab hid the spies in Joshua chapter 2. One reason she was prepared to risk her life in this way was because she, and everyone else around, had heard how the Lord had dried up the Red Sea and brought the Israelites out of Egypt. The resulting fear of the Lord persuaded her to commit the rest of her life to this powerful God.

This name by which God had become well known was that of the God of Abraham, Isaac and Jacob. It was under the covenant God had made with them that he had acted to redeem the Israelites, and we learn in Nehemiah 9:10 that this name 'remains to this day'. Indeed, it also remains to our day, for us too. Not to know him in this way is to cut ourselves off from part of who he is.

There is great honesty in this chapter. When reviewing their past they didn't edit out the bad bits. Repeatedly we are told the people continually failed. They had been stubborn and stiff-necked, a typical Hebrew phrase. In those days bowing down to a king involved more than just a slight nod. To be stiff-necked meant you were refusing to give full honour, displaying instead an attitude that was half-hearted and disrespectful, even proud or rebellious. This was how they had treated the King of Heaven.

Above all, Nehemiah chapter 9 highlights the contrast between their sinfulness and God's continual goodness. To sin was bad enough, but to sin against a God who had done so much for them and treated them so well was far worse, something we should also bear in mind, perhaps even more so in the light of the cross.

This chapter of Nehemiah is a constant see-saw of God's goodness and Israel's disobedience. The cycle was relentless. God was gracious and compassionate but the Israelites were disobedient and rebellious, even blasphemous. Yet God was still gracious and compassionate. Even after they had worshipped the golden calf he still guided them day and night, by pillars of cloud and fire respectively. He provided manna and water on a regular basis, and perhaps most wonderfully of all he ensured their clothes didn't wear out or their feet get swollen.

God's readiness to pardon is amazing and glorious. Time and again he was merciful to them and did not abandon them or allow them to suffer the full consequences of their disobedience. The overall message of this chapter is not how special Israel was, but how special God is. Or rather, Israel *is* special but only because of God's special covenant of love towards them.

In the end, punishment and exile did occur. The repeated warnings were not heeded and God had to act. But Israel recognised that it was their fault and God was not to blame in any way. In 9:33 they confess: 'In all that happened to us, you have been just; you have acted faithfully, while we did wrong.'[1] This is an attitude we need to bear in mind when we are tempted to criticise God over things we don't like. God's actions are always both necessary and just.

There are a few more points to bring out of some of these verses before we leave this chapter. In 9:20 we read that when the Israelites were in the wilderness God gave them his 'good Spirit to instruct them'. The adjective 'good' is a less familiar way of describing God's Spirit. Some translations simply say 'in your goodness' but the Hebrew does contain the words 'spirit' and 'good'. This makes sense, for if God is good so must his Spirit be also. This verse should remind us that one of the primary reasons Jesus sent us the Holy Spirit was to teach us and guide us into all truth (John 16:12-15). Being instructed by God's good Spirit is something we should seek every day if we want to live good lives.

One reason Israel kept falling back into their old ways was that they 'failed to remember' what God had done

---

1. NIV 1984 version.

for them (9:17). We have seen how common the word 'remember' is in the book of Nehemiah, as indeed it is throughout scripture. Let's say again that in biblical terms 'remember' is not the opposite of 'forget'. Rather it is about keeping something in the forefront of your mind so that it makes a difference and leads to action where needed. Do we constantly remember what God has done for us? That is why we should take bread and wine frequently, in remembrance of Jesus' love and sacrifice.

Another issue behind Israel's disobedience was that they had put God's Law behind their backs (9:26). This is a vivid illustration to describe what they had effectively done to God's Law. They had put it out of sight. You can't read something that is behind your back (unless you have eyes in the back of your head!). Where do we put God's Word? Where do we keep it during the week? Is it always in front of our eyes, on a table nearby for instance? If it is somewhere where it can be seen then you might just pick it up and read it more often. Perhaps the Israelites were now reading God's Law more because they realised where they had put it in the past, and what had happened as a result.

Confession is about agreeing with God and coming back into line with what he says, recognising that this is reality and to live otherwise is false. But once you realise this, something has to be done. We said at the start of this chapter that there was a good reason behind this day of prayer and confession, and now we have reached this point, one that required a deep commitment. In this case it involved making a binding decision or covenant. Nehemiah

9:38 says, 'In view of all this', but actually in some versions, and indeed in the original, this verse is really the start of Nehemiah chapter 10. This is where we will start in our next chapter.

Chapter Eleven

Nehemiah Chapter 10

We will now pick up where we left off in our previous chapter with the end of Nehemiah chapter 9, which is actually the start of chapter 10! Once again we see how verse numbers can be ambiguous or unhelpful but, to be fair, in this case 9:38 does act as a link between these two chapters of Nehemiah, putting them together and creating a single longer passage which does benefit from being read as one.

Nehemiah 9:38 begins 'In view of all this', referring to everything that they had just prayed and confessed in the first half of that day, the twenty-fourth day of the seventh month of Tishrei. By the end of this six-hour period, the people had come to a place of decision. They wanted a fresh start and were prepared to make a commitment in order to achieve this. Thus they made a binding agreement or covenant which was to be put in writing and sealed by a large number of their officials and leaders. This, it seems, is how they would occupy the rest of this very full and important day.

It was wonderful that the nation as a whole had arrived at this point of feeling that something had to be done to put right the past. But how was this to be enacted?

A vague promise, or even a list of several promises, is not enough in itself. This can soon become meaningless if it is not established and attested in a more visible and durable way. In Nehemiah's time, people were very familiar with the custom of making a covenant, or rather of 'cutting' a covenant, which was the more literal way of describing the process. In the ancient world a new covenant nearly always involved an animal being sacrificed, or cut into pieces. This reminded those involved that this was a costly business and not one to be taken lightly.

In this case it seems that no animals were sacrificed and no blood was shed, but this was still a serious and solemn affair. The written agreement was to be binding upon everyone and a large number of people were willing to put their name to it and seal it personally. Notice the plural 'seals' in 9:38, indicating that this wasn't just the responsibility of the man at the top.

Everyone knew how important covenants were to God who had already made several in the past. Through Abraham, God had promised several things, including a child of promise leading to many offspring that would become a nation – them! Through Moses and with Israel as a whole, God had given them his Law, or way of living properly in relationship with him (more on this in Part Two of our book). And through King David, God had pledged a future king, or Messiah, who would come from David's family line, and eventually fulfil all promises and bring God's purposes to completion.

So in the first half of Nehemiah chapter 10 we have another list of names! Don't groan! We have already seen that these lists were important then, and even for us now there is a need to know who actually sealed this covenant, if only because of what became of it later.

The list begins with Nehemiah himself, then proceeds in categories, starting with priests (twenty-two of them) and Levites (another seventeen). If you are still wondering what is the difference between a priest and a Levite, then the answer is that the Levites were a tribe of Israelites descended from Levi, one of Jacob's twelve sons, whereas the priests were a group from within that tribe who had responsibilities over certain aspects of the Tabernacle (originally) and later the Temple. So, in summary, all priests were Levites but not all Levites were priests.

After these groups come other leaders and officials, a further forty-four names, making a total of eighty-four in all who signed or sealed the agreement. But it didn't end there. There might not have been room for any more seals on the document but everyone else was involved too. Nehemiah 10:28 mentions 'the rest of the people'. They joined in with their brothers listed earlier, who are now described as nobles (10:29). They were given this title most probably because they were the heads of clans or families and generally took the lead in such matters, rather than being the equivalent of what we think of as nobility in Britain today.

There are several points of interest in these two verses (10:28-29). For a start, there are other priests and Levites who presumably were not 'noble' in the above sense. These are mentioned along with the gatekeepers, singers and other Temple servants which were appointed in Nehemiah chapter 7. But there is another intriguing category referred to here: those who had separated themselves from the surrounding peoples for the sake of the Law of God. It seems that certain non-Israelites were included in this covenant, provided they wanted to make a full commitment to God's Law as given to Israel. On that basis, they could become part of this new society. All that was required, as far as this covenant was concerned, was obedience to the Word of God. It was that which would make the community function as one and remain faithful to the God of Israel.

Also in 10:28 we see that the wives took part in this agreement. There was no exemption for women, nor indeed for children who were able to understand, meaning those old enough to know what they were committing to. Only the very youngest would be excluded.

The seriousness of what they were all entering into is shown by the fact that they agreed to bind themselves with a curse and an oath. This meant that if they did not walk in accordance with God's Law they were prepared to accept being cursed as a form of correction. It may not be entirely clear what form this curse would take or even if the people themselves knew exactly what this might entail, but certainly this was something they understood from their past. Deuteronomy chapter 28, for example, sets out in detail the blessings they could expect in return for obedience as well as the curses for disobedience.

In any case, the Israelites recognised it was not for them to decide what God should, or should not, do if they were to rebel again. In their earlier confession they had declared that in the past every punishment was exactly what they had deserved and in every way God had been just. So they knew they had to accept that God could choose what form that curse should take and how long it should last.

Although the sealing of this written agreement was a very public affair and involved a corporate commitment (each of its clauses begins 'we'), its deeper significance lay at a more personal level. This covenant was ultimately between each individual and God. Just as everyone had done their bit to rebuild the wall, now each individual had to take responsibility for their share in this bigger rebuilding project, that of the people of God. This was now the joint task at hand. There has been no mention of the wall for some time, in fact not since the opening verse of Nehemiah chapter 7, and won't be again until its dedication in chapter 12. The focus is now firmly upon the people of God who will live within the wall or at least nearby.

So what exactly did they commit themselves to? What did this sealed agreement involve in practical terms? When we turn to the contents of this written document, we find it covers several specific areas of life and service, each of which contributed to the dedication of a whole life to God. As what we read here will be spotlighted again by the end of Nehemiah, it is important to go through this carefully and in detail.

Their first promise, found in 10:30, is simply stated but profoundly important. We will not give our daughters in marriage to the peoples around us or take their daughters for our sons. Basically, when it came to marital relationships they would maintain a spiritual purity. They knew that intermarriage with non-Israelites caused immense problems, involving as it inevitably would the admission and worship of pagan gods into their society. It had happened in the past, which in itself served as a warning, so to knowingly put themselves in that position again would be especially unacceptable, however tempting such marriages might appear.

In those days marriages were arranged by the parents, so this is a promise to be made by them. Today the same principle applies but the responsibility lies with the young people who want to marry, and those entrusted to advise and prepare them. Critical to this is an understanding that biblically a marriage is a covenant between the two people involved, as outlined in Malachi 2:14, 'she is your partner, the wife of your marriage covenant'. This will create a stronger bond than anything provided by social expectations, romantic love or a desire for future happiness.

The next promise they made was about being faithful to God in business and commerce (10:31). Trading on a Sabbath or other holy days was forbidden but if a merchant from nearby (a sort of local travelling salesman) turned up on one of these special days it would certainly be very tempting to go against these laws. The intention behind the Sabbath laws was to help preserve their distinctiveness as a people. But is this what they really wanted? Or would they be tempted to compromise, to become more like other nations, knowing that this could easily lead to more compromises? The motive for breaking the Sabbath law was obvious; you could make more money buying and selling on seven days than on six. This part of their binding agreement was about earning a living in ways that honoured God. To this end they also pledged that every seventh year they would give the land a rest (to prevent it being overworked and so less fruitful) and cancel all debts. This last commitment is remarkable. Who would want to do this of their own accord? Ultimately, this could involve a significant sacrifice. In fact, much of what was pledged in 10:31, while it may be for the greater good and the glory of God, could well result in personal loss, or at least less gain.

The rest of Nehemiah chapter 10 is summed up by the final phrase: 'We will not neglect the house of our God.' There were several ways in which they would pledge to do this. Nehemiah 10:32 starts with the phrase 'We assume the responsibility', which in effect translates as 'We will impose upon ourselves'. In other words, to maintain the Temple, this is what we will definitely do.

The first commitment they made was to pay the yearly tax to support the working of the Temple. At this time it was a third of a shekel. It is not clear why this was the required amount then as both earlier and later it was half a shekel. Earlier God had told Moses to collect this amount from every male over the age of twenty for the upkeep of the sanctuary (Exod. 30:13-15, 38:26). Later, in Jesus' time, this was also the price of the Temple tax. When Jesus instructed Peter to catch a fish and look in its mouth, he told his disciple that he would find a coin which would be exactly what was required to pay the Temple tax for both of them (Matt. 17:24-27). Although the Greek text mentions a coin known as a 'stater', usually translated in terms of a drachma, in effect this single coin would be a shekel, sufficient for both Jesus and Peter (which incidentally also tells us that Peter was at least twenty years old at this point). Whereas half a shekel wasn't such a large sum of money for an annual tax in ancient times, being generally the equivalent of about two days' wages, perhaps it had been reduced to a third in Nehemiah's day as times were rather tough!

The people also committed themselves to doing everything else necessary for the upkeep of the Temple. This included making contributions of wood to burn on the altar, offering up their firstborn and firstfruits, as well as bringing the tithe of their crops. All of these would be costly, especially giving up the firstborn of their animals, who may not give birth again. Similarly, there was no guarantee their land would produce much more after the initial firstfruits. Nevertheless, they believed that God was worth it, and so they willingly pledged to give whatever was necessary to make sure they did not 'neglect the house of God'.

This phrase is worth bearing in mind as it will occur again towards the end of Nehemiah. We should also consider what this means for us today, now that we, the people of God, are the equivalent of God's Temple in the past. How do we make sure that we do not 'neglect the house of God'?

Chapter Twelve

Nehemiah Chapter 11

As we now surely realise, the book of Nehemiah is full of lists of names which, although important at the time, does provide a challenge to the modern reader, and indeed to anyone preparing talks on the book. Here, in chapter 11, we are once again confronted with another such list, in this case those who would now settle in Jerusalem as their permanent place of residence. But, as we have seen before, there are always questions which can be asked about even the most mundane parts of scripture, and points of interest which can be drawn out of the text for our consideration today. It seems the main purpose behind this list was to commend the people in it, even to praise them for what they were about to do. We don't hear of these people again, or anywhere else in scripture, but they have gone down in history as playing a key role in that place at that time. As such, we can at least take a few minutes to think about these relatively unknown men and women whose lives God had planned for such a time as that.

Nehemiah chapter 11 concerns the repopulating of the city of Jerusalem now that the wall had been rebuilt. Nehemiah knew that what made a city was not just walls and houses but people living there as a community who, along with their families and neighbours, would secure the city's future and preserve it for generations to come. They would still be building something together, working towards God's greater purposes. No-one really knew this yet, but the whole point behind the rebuilding of Jerusalem was to have a city ready for the coming of their Messiah, and in particular a place where he could teach and ultimately die as the Saviour of the world. This was still several centuries away, but God's plans often start small and take a long time to reach their fulfilment.

One issue for Nehemiah to decide upon was how many people should live there. What would be the optimum size of the new city of Jerusalem? Clearly the size in terms of area was already fixed by the new boundary wall – they weren't going to knock that down and expand anytime soon! The real question was one of viability. A certain number was needed to keep going what had been rebuilt, in particular the Temple.

For more than seventy years, Jerusalem had been nothing but a ghost town. Then over the next eighty years or so it had been slowly repopulated, especially once the Temple had been rebuilt. But for a city to prosper and to be regarded as strong in the eyes of surrounding peoples, it needed to be fully populated. This also had the advantage of providing greater resources for its future defence, just in case of trouble. They hadn't put in all that work just to see some marauding army come and break it down again!

Adding up the figures mentioned in Nehemiah chapter 11 may provide some idea of the number of inhabitants that was seen as necessary to make Jerusalem fully functional again, but we should bear in mind that those listed were only the men. When women and children are included it is thought that the total number who took up residence was around 4,000, which would be about 10 per cent of the Israelites in the land at that time.

Numbers aside, the other main issue was *who* would actually go and live there, and that was a greater problem for Nehemiah to solve. You may think that everyone was clambering to get a place in the big city but in reality that was not the case. In fact, most were reluctant. Living in a small village was often the preferred choice. It was easier for many to make a living in a rural location by working on the land or looking after livestock. This would also be a happier way of life for many. The city with its new wall might seem to offer greater security but equally, you were more likely to be a target for the enemy. Now that Jerusalem was a notable city again there was the fear of attack from whole armies, not just small groups of raiders or thieves. You could be trapped there if the city was besieged, whereas in the countryside you had more chance to flee.

For many, to set up home in Jerusalem could have been quite a challenge, one that would involve some big changes. New inhabitants may have been required to give up land elsewhere and take up some new kind of business. They may have had to leave friends and family behind in their old village, and come to terms with city-based problems, such as making sure the water supply functioned properly. Above all, Jerusalem did not yet look all that glorious and there was still plenty of work to do.

Some no doubt felt that life inside the city would be more restrictive. Living on the outskirts was a better option and more desirable. Those with produce to sell still had easy access to the city population, via those new gates, and if danger did threaten there was always the opportunity to go within the city wall for protection.

Even today, many people who work in a big city such as London opt to live outside in the suburbs or even further afield, choosing to live in the so-called Home Counties and commute rather than face the challenges of life in a large metropolis.

In the ancient world there was often animosity between town and country dwellers, especially if those living in the larger places felt they had been given little choice. Forced repopulation was quite common at times. People could be uprooted at the whim of the emperor or regional king. One example from the time of Jesus was Tiberias on the edge of Lake Galilee. Herod Antipas, son of Herod the Great, built this new city around AD 17 and named it in honour of the Emperor Tiberius. Herod wanted it to become the capital of the Galilee, and it was possibly a very pleasant city in a good location. But to make it work, people had to be forced to go and live there, and many may have resented this. It is noticeable that, according to the Gospels, Jesus who spent much of his time in the Galilean towns and villages, never went to Tiberias.

Now that Jerusalem had a new wall, it was a viable city to live in again. But who would choose to live there? Would you have volunteered? Or weighing up the pros and cons, would you rather have gone back to your old place, somewhere familiar, rather than be a pioneer in the next phase of rebuilding the ancient city?

So Nehemiah had a problem here, another issue to sort out and not an easy one. Here was a further test of his leadership and people skills. Basically, he looked first for volunteers, and it is those who willingly offered to live there that are specially commended in this chapter. This was more than just a superficial vote of thanks for doing something that wasn't particularly popular or a fleeting recognition of their commitment to the cause. The Hebrew word for 'commended' is stronger than that. It means they were praised or lauded for making this decision. In fact, literally, it says the people blessed them. For being prepared to endure possible hardship and discomfort in order to accomplish an even greater work for God, they received the blessing of others. This is a wonderful way to reward someone for their service to others and to God. Perhaps we should look to bless our brothers and sisters more in return for what they do for each of us in the name of the Lord?

It is also notable that all the main leaders settled in Jerusalem (11:1). Presumably these were the same people who had sealed the written agreement in Nehemiah chapter 10. It was important that they set the right example. Their position put them under a certain obligation. They had no right to expect others to come and inhabit Jerusalem if they themselves were not living there.

Some of the provincial leaders from towns in the territories of Judah and Benjamin also now had their homes in the city, as inevitably so did some of the priests and Levites. Many were there to oversee the practical tasks needed to maintain the house of God both physically and spiritually (11:16-17).

But all these, together with those that had volunteered, was still not sufficient to make the city a viable one, so Nehemiah held a ballot to make up the required number, choosing one of out every ten. It seems that everyone accepted both the process and the outcome as there were no complaints before or afterwards, at least that we know of. So again Nehemiah had shown wisdom in finding an acceptable solution to a tricky dilemma.

Once the ballot was over, the others could go back to their ancestral homes in the provinces. Some of the settlements named are already familiar to us or easily recognisable today. For instance, there is reference in 11:35 to Ono, which featured in Nehemiah chapter 6 as the place where Sanballat and Geshem hoped to lure Nehemiah, presumably to harm him in some way. We saw then that the plain of Ono was a long way from Jerusalem, some 20 miles to the west of the city. Others must also have lived some distance away from Jerusalem as indicated in 11:30, where it mentions those living all the way from Beersheba to the Valley of Hinnom.

The Valley of Hinnom was just outside Jerusalem, situated to the south and west of the city, with the Valley Gate named after it. Beersheba is well known in the Bible mainly through the stories of the patriarchs, and in particular because of a well dug there by Abraham, which gave the place its name, meaning 'well of the oath' (see Gen. 21:31). Beersheba became known as the southernmost limit of the land and the phrase 'From Dan to Beersheba' became the usual, almost proverbial, way of designating the whole length of the Promised Land (see Judg. 20:1, 2 Sam. 24:2,

1 Chron. 21:2). This has been calculated as a total distance of about 140 miles. Even from Beersheba to Jerusalem the direct distance is over 40 miles and probably more like 60 miles by road. From this alone we can see that many who took part in rebuilding Jerusalem would eventually live far away and would probably only get to see it again if they travelled there for special occasions such as the feast days.

Others did live much nearer, for instance the Temple servants, who obviously needed a much shorter journey to work. In 11:21 we read that they lived on the hill of Ophel, which was a small fortified settlement on a ridge to the east of the city near the Temple area. The name means 'fortified hill' or 'risen area'.

Another intriguing feature of these verses is the mention in 11:24 of Pethahiah, who was of the tribe of Judah but who is also described as the king's agent in all affairs relating to the people. This king was, of course, Artaxerxes, so it seems he had a special agent or official working for him among the Israelites, presumably to oversee the king's business there, including the collecting of taxes. In the previous verse (v. 23), even the singers responsible for the service of the house of God were under the king's orders. These orders regulated the daily activity of the Temple singers, so perhaps Pethahiah had some role in that regard too.

There are often so many small details in chapters like this which we never fully understand. So much remains in the past. But the more we study passages such as Nehemiah chapter 11 the clearer the bigger picture becomes and we realise that what seems to be merely a list of names can actually be quite fascinating.

At least I hope so, as there is yet another one coming up next in Nehemiah chapter 12. But this chapter also features another very big day of celebration in the life of the restored city, namely the long-awaited dedication of the wall. So there is much to look forward to!

Chapter Thirteen

Nehemiah Chapter 12

As warned at the end of our last chapter, we are about to meet yet another list of names, though at least this does not occupy the whole of Nehemiah chapter 12. In this case, many of the names are from their past, so it is worth asking why they feature at all at this point in the book of Nehemiah.

In general, connecting with the past can be helpful for understanding the present and for anticipating the future. This is why it is often part of a major celebratory event to look back and remember what has gone before, to see what has led up to this significant moment in time. In particular it is good to think of those whose contributions in the past have helped to create the current circumstances, and recognise that without them the present-day occasion may not be happening at all.

In this case, the big event of the day was the dedication of the newly built wall of Jerusalem and although everyone had played some part in its construction, the ceremony would be mainly led by the priests and especially the Levites. In some ways this could be seen as the climax of decades of service by these two groups, so it was right to go back into the historical records (or 'the book of the annals' as it is called in 12:23) and recall the family histories of those alive at that time.

The first part of the list (12:1-9), names the priests and Levites who came back in the first return of 537 BC under Zerubbabel and Joshua the high priest (here named as Jeshua). Jeshua's son, Joiakim, heads up the next part of the list from 12:12 onwards. It is thought from some sources that Joiakim may have been the next high priest after Joshua, though this is by no means certain. But clearly this is the next generation of priests and Levites, and the phrase 'in the days of Joiakim' must have been readily understood as a particular piece of history leading up to the time of Darius I (522 to 486 BC), when the next grouping occurs from 12:22 onwards.

We have seen previously that a list of names can be fascinating and passages like this often contain small details which add to the bigger picture. However, our main concern here is what took place on this special day of dedication rather than a close look at this recital of names from the past. But before we move on, let's just pick out one. In 12:4 there is a mention of Iddo. Is that a familiar name to you? Look further down the list and he occurs again in 12:16 where we also find that he was related to a man named Zechariah. Now there are plenty of Zechariahs in scripture (about thirty in all), but, yes, this is the one we know from a later book in the Old Testament. In Zechariah 1:1 we learn that the prophet Zechariah was the grandson of Iddo. The lineage mentioned in the opening verse of this book marks him out precisely as the same person, which is why such genealogies can be helpful in making connections.

The opening of the book of Zechariah is dated as the second year of Darius, which is around 520 or 521 BC. This also puts it in the right time period. But what is interesting here is that the prophet Zechariah was also a priest; in fact he was one of the heads of the priestly families (12:12). It was extremely rare to find someone who was both prophet and priest. Perhaps this is the only significant case (before Jesus, that is).

Clearly, Zechariah was just one priest among many (about two in every fifteen of those who returned from exile was from a priestly background), but his calling as a prophet was unique. He had a long prophetic ministry, unlike his contemporary, Haggai, whose ministry lasted just four months within a single year. Zechariah brought a series of short messages or visions over a period of two years (520 to 518 BC) and then after a gap of what may have been several decades, he spoke twice more, giving two lengthy oracles, or burdens, which are apocalyptic in nature and vital to our understanding of the future.

Incidentally, the name Zechariah means 'God remembers', which we have seen is a common theme in Nehemiah, and an important part of understanding God's nature, which might explain the popularity of the name. His father's name, Berekiah, means 'God blesses', and Iddo means 'his appointed time'. Looking up what a name means can often be instructive.

It is a shame that the way our Bible is usually arranged means that we struggle to connect both Haggai and Zechariah to the time of Ezra-Nehemiah, and may even miss the link completely. The main point here, though, is that, despite his importance and uniqueness as a prophet, in Nehemiah chapter 12 Zechariah is simply slipped into a list of names of a larger group of those with a priestly function, who together played an important part in the build-up to the dedication of the wall of Jerusalem.

From 12:27 onwards, we read about this special day of celebration. But first, those to be involved had to be gathered together from where they lived and brought into Jerusalem. We saw previously that many of the priests and Levites did not live in Jerusalem but had returned to their ancestral property in the many towns of Judah (11:20). We now learn that the singers had done likewise and in fact had even previously built villages for themselves around Jerusalem (12:29). It seems that these singers had decided to form their own close-knit communities and this may well have helped them develop bonds of fellowship, which in turn enhanced their service to God in worship.

But such living arrangements in themselves were not enough. Something else was needed by way of preparation, namely purification. The priests and Levites had to purify themselves ceremonially first, otherwise they could not lead the people. Their next task was to purify the rest of the people, and then in this case the gates and the wall.

Ritual purification, or ceremonial washing, was an important part of Judaism then, especially prior to worship or attending the Temple. This may seem strange to us today, especially if we don't understand the idea of ritual uncleanness. This is nothing to do with being physically dirty or morally sinful. It was usually required following childbirth or during menstruation, or other occasions associated with bodily fluids, as well as situations that involved skin diseases or coming into contact with a dead body (human or animal). So there may have been health aspects to this as well but that was not its primary objective. Whether by simply washing the hands or by full immersion in a *mikveh* bath, this was a ritual or ceremony whose main purpose was to make the participant think how different it was to be human rather than God. God doesn't give birth or have problems with his skin, so whenever this happened within human life this was an opportunity for a greater recognition that God is radically distinct from us, which should in turn prepare us better for worship. Taking part in a purification process was also a matter of being obedient to God on a regular basis. Overall, we would do well to think through what still might be required of us before we approach a holy God in worship or celebration.

We can see from 12:31, and later in verses 38 and 40, that this part of the book is now based upon Nehemiah's personal memoirs, not historical records. The use of 'I' twice in 12:31 shows that Nehemiah himself had made the arrangements and taken responsibility for the event. Everything that was to happen that day was done according to his instructions and under his leadership. From the other uses of the personal pronoun 'I' (verses 38 and 40) we see that Nehemiah personally took part in the procession by following one the choirs, joining in with half of the people. He was not standing apart at a distance watching it all happen, overseeing it with a sense of pride and personal achievement. But we can imagine that with each step he took he probably felt a certain amount of satisfaction and triumph. He wouldn't have been human otherwise. But maybe his overwhelming feeling was one of gratitude to Almighty God. Perhaps he thought back to that day in Susa when he first heard from Hanani and others that Jerusalem was in trouble and disgrace, with its wall broken down and its gates burnt to ashes. After a long journey and a monumental effort, here was a moment to savour.

If gratitude was Nehemiah's primary emotion, that would explain why the main feature of the day he had organised was that of thanksgiving. To that end, two large choirs had been assembled, which were to process in opposite directions to each other, one going round the wall clockwise, the other anticlockwise.

The text suggests that they did this on top of the wall (12:38), though there is an alternative (footnote) translation of 'alongside' it. In many ways 'on top' seems much more preferable. Do you remember that taunt of Tobiah in Nehemiah 4:3 that 'even a fox climbing up on it would break down their wall of stones!'? To march along the top of the wall would demonstrate what a good job they had done. We've got a wall now, not just a pile of rubble – and look how strong it is! Perhaps they also remembered the time in their history when their ancestors had marched around the much larger and stronger walls of Jericho and brought them crashing down. Not so here!

What about the practicality of being on top? The width of the wall (around 2.5 metres) was sufficient provided they were disciplined enough to remain in line (no accidents, please, this is meant to be a happy day!). Getting up there, around 12 metres, might have proved a bit of a challenge, but we have seen that Nehemiah had overcome bigger challenges than this in the past. It seems the day passed without undue incident, so perhaps Nehemiah could add stage management and choreography to his set of skills.

Both choirs set off from the same place, the Valley Gate, which is where Nehemiah had begun his preliminary tour of the wall one night, three days after arriving in Jerusalem (see Neh. 2:11ff). The first choir headed south past the Dung Gate, continuing anticlockwise as far as the Water Gate. Nehemiah 12:37 does suggest they were on top of the wall for at least some of the way. Reference is made to going up some steps on the ascent to the wall and passing above the house of David. The second choir set off clockwise, going north, taking in the Fish Gate and the Sheep Gate, eventually stopping at the Gate of the Guard. Both choirs then came together again to take their places in the Temple.

What a sight this 'two choirs festival' must have been, and what a sound they made! Not only was there singing, which may have been antiphonal, meaning that the two choirs sung alternately in response to each other, but there were also musical instruments to add to the joyful sound. Specifically mentioned are trumpets (either shofars or silver trumpets) as well as others not named here but which had been specified for worship in the past by King David. Most notably these would be cymbals, stringed instruments and harps, but there are over twenty different musical instruments mentioned in the Bible so there may have been others too. It is interesting to see David mentioned at this point and still revered as 'the man of God' (12:36, see also v. 24). In particular, this is another example of the Israelites wanting to get back in line with their past (even their glory days) and start to do things again in the way that God had ordained.

Nehemiah 12:43 is significant for two reasons. Firstly, the emphasis on the joy of this day. There are four mentions of joy or rejoicing in this one verse alone. Even the women and children rejoiced! No-one was left out. Everyone was taken up with joy and thanksgiving because of all that God had done for them.

Secondly, this verse also states that the sound of their rejoicing carried a long way, far beyond the city itself. Again, if the choirs were on top of the wall then this would help. Their worship was also a testimony. Others who were not part of this occasion would know what it meant to the Israelites. This would include their enemies who had tried to prevent the building of the wall. Imagine what they were now feeling when they heard all this. Their defeat was complete.

So too our worship should be a testimony to others of the greatness of our God, which is why we should choose our songs carefully, making sure they are God-centred and Bible-focused. In particular, genuine praise and worship will have a strong element of thanksgiving to God, and be full of joy so that others catch the excitement of being in God's presence, all the while remembering that the goal isn't to give people a good feeling (though that may happen), but to give glory and honour to God.

In the final verses of chapter 12 (verses 44-47) we find that appointments were made to oversee the storerooms for the various offerings, firstfruits and tithes that were set apart for the priests and Levites. The people were happy to make these contributions for we read that Judah was pleased with their ministry. The singers and gatekeepers also received daily portions in return for their service as the Israelites in general returned to the practices that God had ordained in the past via commands given to them through David and Solomon.

Also on that day the Book of Moses was read aloud to the people, but that belongs to the final chapter of Nehemiah, where we must tackle the challenges that this chapter throws up and in particular the issue of chronology. What really happened at the end, and when?

Chapter Fourteen

Nehemiah Chapter 13

We have reached the final chapter of the book of Nehemiah, where we encounter the rather sad and strange way in which the book ends. There are some troubling incidents to comment upon, and as we said previously we cannot avoid tackling the challenges that Nehemiah chapter 13 throws up and in particular the issue of chronology. What really happened at the end, and when?

In some ways it is upsetting that this chapter occurs at all. Why can't the final part of the book be the end of chapter 12 with verses 44 to 47, or even better at 12:43 with all that rejoicing that could be heard for miles? But the Bible is always an honest book. If problems arise or things go wrong, it tells us. We need to know about these and, above all, try to understand why. That way we appreciate better the human condition, and also realise how God must feel at times.

And what about Nehemiah? How did he feel about the things we read in this chapter? But we must start with a chronological conundrum. Where exactly was Nehemiah when some of these things happened? In Jerusalem or back in Susa? Let's try to put the pieces of the puzzle together.

We know from Nehemiah 13:6 that Nehemiah at some point returned to Susa and went back into the service of King Artaxerxes. This makes sense as he had not resigned his post as cupbearer, he had merely asked for an indefinite leave of absence for a particular task. Now that task had been fulfilled he must have felt an obligation to go back to Susa which was, after all, his home. He could easily have packed his bags and made his travel arrangements as soon as the wall had been dedicated and the celebrations were over. But did he? Or did he stay for longer, much longer?

Also by then, he had appointed everyone he needed to – gatekeepers, singers, Levites, residents as guards and he had even put his brother Hanani in charge of Jerusalem (Neh. 7:1-3). He had organised the repopulation of the city, checked that the Law was being read, and overseen the celebrations of the day of dedication. After all that, he could return home happy and report back to the King of Persia how well it had all gone (mostly).

But it seems he didn't leave then. In fact it appears he stayed for the full twelve-year span mentioned in the book as being from the twentieth to the thirty-second year of the reign of Artaxerxes. This can be seen from Nehemiah 13:6, where it is stated clearly, but also deduced earlier from 5:14 when Nehemiah says that for this whole period he did not eat the food usually allotted to the governor. So the common assumption that Nehemiah's first visit to Jerusalem lasted for twelve years seems the best option.

But in which case why did he go back *then*? What prompted him to return after so long? And did things only start to go wrong *after* he left? If his absence was part of the reason for the decline and disobedience, then that is worth noting and considering further.

138

Then we learn from Nehemiah 13:6-7 that, having returned to Susa, Nehemiah at some point asked the king once again for permission to go back to Jerusalem, and this was granted. How long he was in Susa before he made this request is not recorded; the text simply says 'some time later', which is rather vague but which suggests a few months rather than several years, otherwise there would most likely have been an indication in which year in the reign of Artaxerxes this took place. So overall, given that the journey time was at least three months each way, the consensus is that Nehemiah may have been away from Jerusalem for a year or so but maybe not that much more.

There is a significant point behind all this, namely how quickly things changed for the worse back in Jerusalem; how swift was the decline and re-emergence of past failings. If Nehemiah had left once the walls were completed and stayed away much longer, then we could say it was a slow decline. But if, as seems more likely, Nehemiah stayed in Jerusalem for the longer period (twelve years) and then was away for only a short time (say, one year), then the decline was rapid. How quickly can things go wrong? Very, seems to be the answer.

Also intriguing is that no reason is given as to why, once he was back in Susa, Nehemiah decided to return to Jerusalem. Had Hanani come rushing over with more reports of trouble and disgrace? It seems not. There is no mention of anyone this time visiting Nehemiah with news about the city or the people. In fact, it is clear that only when he was back in Jerusalem did Nehemiah learn about some of the things that had gone wrong (Neh. 13:7, 10).

It also seems that Nehemiah himself may have uncovered certain problems. In 13:15 and 13:23 we find the phrase

'In those days', which clearly refers to his time back in Jerusalem. In these instances, Nehemiah declared, 'I saw men in Judah', and then described the various things they were doing, suggesting that he personally came across these acts of wrongdoing. He saw them for himself rather than having been told about them beforehand.

We may wonder if Nehemiah at some point wished he hadn't come back to Jerusalem at all and seen these things. It would have been a perfectly normal reaction. Perhaps also he began to blame himself for leaving when he did. Is this my fault in any way? Did I get it right before, or did I make mistakes, even unwittingly? We may want to consider this a bit more later on.

But we haven't quite finished with our conundrum of chronology yet. There are some other pieces of the puzzle to examine, namely the various phrases that seem to act as time-based markers. These start in Nehemiah 12:44 with 'At that time' and continue with 'On that day' (13:1), 'Before this' (13:4), and Nehemiah's crucial statement in 13:6, 'While *all this* was going on, I was not in Jerusalem' (italics mine). All what?

Presumably Nehemiah *was* in Jerusalem at the time that men were appointed to the various roles mentioned in Nehemiah 12:44, and on the day that the book of Moses was read aloud in Nehemiah 13:1, especially if this was the same day as the dedication of the wall which we know he attended. In fact, the Hebrew phrase 'at that time' in Nehemiah 12:44 is literally 'on that day' and is identical to that in 13:1. Both involve the Hebrew word '*yom*' which can mean a literal day or not, but most likely does so in this case as the passage is referring to the specific day of dedication. All these events, the appointments and the public reading of the Law, were part of that celebration. In which case, Nehemiah was present when the problem mentioned in Nehemiah 13:1-3 was discovered and he may well have been involved in resolving this, though he is not mentioned by name in 13:3. Perhaps this was the last thing Nehemiah did, if indeed he did go back to Susa soon after the celebrations, but if, as we have seen is more likely, he stayed on for many years, then at this point it would seem that everything was now in order and remained so for some time.

But then what do we make of the phrase 'Before this' (13:4)? Does this mean that the problems with Tobiah, which Eliashib had allowed, had taken place previously, while Nehemiah was still governor of the city? In which case, had Nehemiah been complacent or negligent here? Had he turned a blind eye to what was going on or, worse, was he complicit in this? But if, as 13:7 implies, these events were part of the 'all this' which was going on while he was not in Jerusalem, how then do we read verses 4 and 5?

There are two points to be made here. Firstly, the phrase 'before this' could refer simply to Eliashib being put in charge of the storerooms. It was his *appointment* that had taken place previously, not his misdemeanours. In which case, this means that Eliashib assumed his position of authority before those others who are mentioned in Nehemiah 12:44. After all, we know from Nehemiah 3:1 that Eliashib was the high priest, so it makes sense if he was appointed in overall charge first and others later.

In which case Nehemiah is guilty, but only of being a poor judge of character, of failing to realise that Eliashib was maybe not that trustworthy after all. Eliashib's close links with Tobiah, one of those previously opposed to rebuilding the wall, should have rung alarm bells. And there had been indications even after the wall had been completed that Tobiah was still a disreputable character and a likely troublemaker (see Neh. 6:17-19). Nehemiah could blame himself a little here. With more foresight he could have prevented this situation developing.

However, a second point can be made based upon a different understanding of 'before this'. The Hebrew phrase is usually translated in a *temporal* sense, 'before' meaning 'previously in time'. However, it can also be taken in a *positional* sense, 'before' meaning 'in front of' as in 'I stand before you'. In which case, what is mentioned in Nehemiah 13:4-5 is being declared to be 'in the forefront' of all that was going wrong. In other words, this was very serious, even more so than the other problems found in this chapter, perhaps because it involved the high priest himself or because it took place within the house of God. From this point of view, the events of Nehemiah 13:4-5 could have occurred much later but were to be seen as more severe in their impact. It was a matter of *consequence* rather than *sequence*. Other things could have gone wrong first, but this was the epitome of it all, and it was really bad.

This view is underlined by Nehemiah's reaction in 13:8; he was 'greatly displeased'. This is a typical Jewish understatement. The wording is actually much stronger: he grieved bitterly and was extremely furious. He also took severe action, throwing all Tobiah's possessions out of the Temple room which Eliashib had provided for him. He then set about purifying or cleansing the room so it could be restored to its sacred use.

We have spent a lot of time on textual technicalities over timing, which I hope has been sufficiently clear. So far we haven't mentioned many of the actual problems themselves. We've been sorting out to what extent Nehemiah may or may not have been responsible for at least some of them. But this has been important as it reflects on his character and integrity. In particular, we see a contrast between two leaders: Nehemiah and Eliashib. The latter, a key spiritual leader in Israel, had abused his position, giving favours which weren't his to give. Tobiah was an Ammonite and should not even have been allowed in the Temple let alone be provided with a room there for his personal use. On top of that, here was a man who had a history of actively opposing God's work. Favouring him was a sure way of sowing seeds of disaster.

As for Nehemiah, all this must have been quite devastating. Did he think he had failed by not putting leadership in place who would operate according to godly principles when he was not there? Did he begin to question the lasting value of any spiritual revival when it could all be reversed so quickly and easily? If so, he soon put these thoughts to one side and began to address the various situations, often quite forcefully. Action was needed, not self-doubt or melancholic introspection.

Let's now focus briefly on the other problems mentioned in this chapter. What had gone wrong? In short, everything! Perhaps this is best summed up by Nehemiah's question in 13:11, 'Why is the house of God neglected?' This is a powerful question given the written agreement made in chapter 10 following their confession in chapter 9. Look again at this agreement (Neh. 10:28-39) and note especially that it ended with their promise that 'We will not neglect the house of our God'.

They had promised not to engage in marriage with foreign women, but this they were now doing again (13:23-27). They had promised not to trade on the Sabbath, but this they were now doing again (13:15-22). They had promised to support the Temple, pay their tithes and bring in their firstfruits, but this they were not now doing (13:10). Israel was again steeped in exactly the same sins that they had confessed before and vowed to stop.

Let's pick up some specific points from these verses and also consider how Nehemiah dealt with these issues.

Regarding Sabbath trading, Nehemiah realised part of the problem was that the gatekeepers weren't doing their job. Local Judeans as well as those outside the community of Israel, such as men from Tyre who lived there, were turning up at the city gates on a Sabbath and being allowed in to trade. So Nehemiah ordered the gates be kept shut on a Sabbath and placed new gatekeepers in charge, as well as commanding the Levites to guard the gates on the Sabbath. When Nehemiah noticed some traders hanging about all night outside the wall he threatened them with some form of physical punishment. We can assume that 'lay hands on you' was not an offer of prayer or ministry (13:21)! We have noted before the importance of the gates and the gatekeepers, and here we see one example why this is so. We should think what this might mean for us, which is why we return to this theme in Part Two of this book.

Regarding marrying foreign women, we see in 13:24 another likely consequence beyond that of introducing pagan gods into their worship. Children learnt to speak from their mother and so were likely to pick up foreign languages rather than learn Hebrew fluently. Over time this might mean the reading and understanding of the Torah could diminish, introducing another future risk, so Nehemiah again acted immediately and forcefully. For us 13:25 might seem rather alarming or quite humorous. The Living Bible translates this as, 'So I confronted these parents and cursed them and punched a few of them and knocked them around and pulled out their hair.' This approach to church discipline may not be included today in leadership courses or manuals of pastoral techniques, but from Nehemiah's strong reaction we see how dangerous he considered such sins to be. So ought we.

As well as giving up one of the Temple rooms to Tobiah, Eliashib had also not been overseeing the storerooms properly or ensuring that the Levites and singers were receiving the portions assigned to them. As a result, these key Temple workers had been forced back to their own fields to work on the land for a living. Temple worship had therefore suffered and again Nehemiah had to set the situation right. He rebuked those responsible for letting this happen and put new people in place to ensure that 'normal service' was resumed.

As we have seen, Eliashib's close association with Tobiah was one major problem, but another involved Eliashib's own family. Sanballat, one of the Israelites' main enemies and a chief opponent of the rebuilding of the wall, was actually related to Eliashib by marriage. One of the high priest's grandsons (a son of Joiada) had married one of Sanballat's daughters. Not only was this a forbidden foreign marriage (Sanballat was a Moabite) but it had defiled the priestly office and the covenant of the priesthood and of the Levites (13:29).

Whether this marriage had just happened during Nehemiah's absence or whether this is something he should have known about before is not stated, but Nehemiah's response is again decisive. The phrase 'I drove him away from me' (13:28) suggests expulsion of some kind, perhaps from the priesthood. But who exactly is meant by 'him'? This could be said to be ambiguous. Was it just the unnamed grandson, the guilty son of Joiada? Or could it refer to Joiada or even Eliashib himself for allowing this to happen? Either way, once again the issue was dealt with immediately and severely.

We have skipped over the opening three verses of the chapter as this issue was tackled in Chapter Four of this book, and, as we said earlier, this most likely took place before Nehemiah returned to Susa. Clearly a lot had gone on during his absence. Many positions had been abused, and compromises made. It does make you wonder once again if Nehemiah had been away for much longer than just a year or so, but once sin and error sets in again it can spread quickly.

Nehemiah chapter 13 is usually described as Nehemiah's final reforms. Basically it involves a series of confrontations, but always backed up with prayer. Four times we find one of those short arrow prayers that Nehemiah used frequently (13:14, 22, 29, 31). Each starts with that powerful word, 'remember'. Overall this was a period of trauma and doubt for Nehemiah, but he knew that God was still with him and that if he did what was right then God would continue to act on his behalf.

There are a few more comments to come out of chapter 13, plus some extra general thoughts on the book as a whole, so we will pick these up in the next chapter as we round off Part One.

Chapter Fifteen

Conclusion

In this chapter we will be saying a bit more about the ending of the book of Nehemiah, in particular *why* it concludes as it does. We will also pick up on a few extra thoughts that have emerged out of the 'conversations' we have had with this part of our Bible.

Let's go back to the beginning, and Nehemiah's request to King Artaxerxes to let him go to Jerusalem to rebuild the wall. Nehemiah himself is, of course, central to the whole book. We have seen his faithfulness and integrity, and noted how remarkable it was that he remained steadfast in the face of continual opposition and fierce attacks upon both himself and the people. But there is a back story to this which we find in the companion book of Ezra, which is a sort of prequel to Nehemiah, an account of what happened beforehand. Take time at some point to read through Ezra chapter 4 which is about the various kinds of opposition to God's work before Nehemiah came on the scene but which contains some interesting similarities.

Ezra chapter 4 starts by explaining there was opposition to the rebuilding of the Temple (4:1-5). One tactic by Israel's enemies was to offer to join in this task, presumably in order to disrupt it. But they are told they can have no part in this. 'We alone will build it for the LORD' (4:3). This might remind you of Nehemiah's response to the initial opposition he faced (Neh. 2:20). But in Ezra we read that their enemies continued to successfully discourage the people and frustrate the work over a long period, from the reign of Cyrus to that of Darius. Although the foundations of the Temple had been laid, work on the rest of the Temple stopped until the second year of Darius, around 521 BC (Ezra 4:24).

Of greater interest to us is the section in Ezra chapter 4 verses 6 to 23 which is an interlude within Ezra's main account of the rebuilding of the Temple. He wants us to know more about the kind of opposition the Israelites repeatedly faced over many years, so he skips ahead to the time of Xerxes (486 BC) and Artaxerxes (465 BC). This is the same Artaxerxes we find in Nehemiah but earlier in his reign. The book of Nehemiah begins in the twentieth year of his reign, so Ezra chapter 4 may be recording events long before Nehemiah was his cupbearer. He may not even have been working in the palace yet, or indeed working anywhere given we don't know anything about his age.

But read Ezra 4:7-23 carefully and certain interesting facts emerge. By then the Temple was now rebuilt so they could, indeed should, begin restoring the walls and repairing the foundations of the city. But this also drew fierce opposition, just as it would do in Nehemiah's day. Here, the opposition was from different people and took the form of a letter to the king (4:7), but some of the accusations are similar. With secure walls they will rebel against you! Jerusalem has a past record of this. If you, Artaxerxes, let them rebuild then you will lose taxes and influence in the whole Trans-Euphrates area (4:12-16).

The plan worked. Artaxerxes issued an order to force them to stop rebuilding the wall, but notice in 4:21 that he left it slightly open. 'This city will not be rebuilt *until I so order*' (italics mine). He reserved the right to change his mind which clearly he did once Nehemiah approached him several years later.

So with this background, we can now read the opening of Nehemiah in a new light. Previous opposition had halted any rebuilding in the past, and would have disheartened the people. Nehemiah must eventually have realised all this, perhaps even before Hanani arrived from Jerusalem with his report, and he would have known that it was Artaxerxes, his master, who had given in to these demands and decreed that the rebuilding must stop. Was this partly why Nehemiah was very much afraid to approach the king on this matter (Neh. 2:2)? But somehow, with God's help, he was able to change the king's mind. Perhaps he knew of that little clause 'until I so order', and understood that this time of 'until' had now arrived. Opposition might remain and be tough at times, but circumstances had changed, so this time it would not succeed.

Let's now return to that strange and in some ways rather unsettling ending to the book of Nehemiah. Chapter 13 is almost like a postscript, one we might wish had been left unwritten. But it's there and we must come to terms with it. There's actually a lot we can learn from this final chapter, especially if we bear in mind that Nehemiah belongs right at the end of the Old Testament. From that point of view, this chapter brings their recorded history to a close, at least for 400 years. Not that they knew it then. But we have hindsight and can use this wonderful benefit to draw some useful lessons.

We've already discussed in our previous chapter at what point Nehemiah might have returned to Susa and then come back to Jerusalem again, and how devastating it was for him when he realised it had all gone wrong in his absence. Did he feel let down by those he had left in charge? Or did he carry a sense of personal failure? After all, he had made those appointments. Perhaps he should have been more discerning. Or maybe it had been too much of a one-man show, and they had relied too heavily on him, so it fell apart when he was not there. There was much there for him to ponder, but on reflection he might have realised something quite different, namely the inevitability of it all.

From their history it was clear that no amount of Law reading, renewed vows or rededication was ever a guarantee of future obedience. There was a repeated pattern here, all through their scripture. The classic case, and perhaps the most extreme, was when Moses came back down the mountain from the presence of God carrying the two tablets of the Law, only to find the Israelites dancing in idolatrous worship round a self-made calf of gold. And all this led by his trusted second-in-command and elder brother, Aaron! Check out Exodus chapter 32 for the details, and note in particular 32:7-8 where God pre-warned Moses of this before he descended back down the mountain: 'They have been quick to turn away from what I have commanded them ...'

Poor Moses. And he soon realised how prevalent this would be. By the end of his ministry, just before he died and, probably thankfully, handed over the baton to Joshua, Moses arranged for the regular reading of the Law but at the same time predicted that rebellion would be commonplace in the future (see Deuteronomy chapter 31). Now Nehemiah would have known all this and perhaps took some consolation from it. If that was Moses' experience, why should it be any different for him?

Interestingly, the apostle Paul went through the same thing time and time again. He would make converts, establish a church, teach them the basics, appoint elders to look after them and then leave, only later to receive letters full of problems to be sorted out. Paul knew that everything written in the Old Testament was there to teach us (Rom. 15:4). Isn't it wonderful to think of the apostle drawing lessons from Nehemiah like we're doing, and probably taking comfort from the fact that the troubles in the churches weren't necessarily all his fault!?

The book of Nehemiah ends by pointing to failure. We might have hoped for better after all the hardship, prayer and toil. But instead it acts as yet another reminder that new structures and renewed vows can in themselves do nothing to transform the perverse inclinations of the human heart. This anti-climax of an ending does not discount all the efforts made but it does once again expose the weaknesses of all mankind, even those who are called the people of God. In addition it acts as a caution against placing too much confidence in church reform or mighty leaders as though these in themselves might ultimately change human nature. Only the grace of God can do this.

So here at the end of Old Testament history, Nehemiah is pulling out hair – probably his own as well as others. But he could never have fixed the people in the way that he fixed the wall. People are not inanimate objects, to be placed in position never to move again. They have a will of their own. So we must not expect to find in Nehemiah a reform programme that would work for all time. What is needed instead?

Effectively, even if somewhat implicitly, the book of Nehemiah preaches Christ, or perhaps we should say the need for a Messianic intervention. This is what God's people had been waiting for ever since the first disobedience. This goes back to Genesis 3:15 when God promised that one of Eve's offspring would one day come and crush the head of the evil one who had brought disobedience and rebellion into God's good creation. Here was the promise that could not fail, but as Nehemiah closes they were still waiting for this and would have to do so for another 400 years.

We are now historically on the other side of this promise. Christ has come. But the message of Nehemiah remains. If we could be rescued from our own failings by simply making more promises of our own, then Christ's death would have been noble but unnecessary. We aren't saved by some vow we make or some leaf we turn over, but by trusting in the Promised One and what he has done for us. As part of this we have to learn to distrust ourselves and our own efforts, and at times maybe even our own institutions and systems, and those who lead them. The book of Nehemiah is part of that lesson.

As with any single book of the Bible, Nehemiah exhorts us to take the macroscopic view of scripture, to recognise the bigger picture, to see the whole story and where it is going. Each book provides just one scene in the mighty drama which stretches from the beginning of time to the start of the eternal age. We need to understand where Nehemiah fits into all this.

There may be no scripture immediately following Nehemiah, no further direct revelation for a long time, but God's story continues, even in the gaps. Long periods of time are no problem to God as he works out his plans and ultimate purpose. The end of Nehemiah should leave us wanting more. What is the next stage? Surely the whole story can't end like this?

Perhaps we need to understand these hidden years better, those centuries between Nehemiah and the birth of that promised offspring of Eve. Here is something worth exploring. Taking a journey through that waiting time between the testaments will help us to make stronger biblical connections and better prepare us to enter the world of Jesus.

We would also benefit from looking at the history of Jerusalem as a whole, its role and significance over the centuries, including the present and the future. Then we might see the bigger context of the work that Nehemiah and the Israelites did at that time.

In particular, the book of Nehemiah should lead us to ask why they were rebuilding Jerusalem at all. Why was it important to restore the city? Was it just for them to reconnect with their past and make a new start for themselves? Or was there a bigger reason?

Little did they realise it at the time, but they were actually starting to prepare a city in readiness for the promised Messiah, a place where God's Son would come to teach and to die, in order to deal with those issues of disobedience and rebellion which so beset them. This was God's bigger purpose behind all their efforts.

When we look into the book of Nehemiah to find principles for rebuilding, whether it is our own lives, our church or our community, we need that bigger perspective. *Why* are we doing these things? Is it so that Jesus can come into our midst to teach, to heal, to be worshipped? In addition, do we also realise that we should be building in readiness for his return to planet Earth and in particular to reign from Jerusalem? In all we do, we should be preparing ourselves to be his bride, to spend eternity with him and ultimately enter a New Jerusalem. This is not about expounding any particular end-time theology, just having a better sense of our future, where we are heading, and capturing the vision given at the end of the whole Bible story in the book of Revelation.

Everything that the Israelites were doing in Nehemiah in that period of history, they were doing for Jesus' sake. They just didn't realise it. Do we? We can be so preoccupied with our wall, our city, our lives, our church that we become blind to what this is ultimately all for.

If reading the final chapter of Nehemiah conveys a sense of desperation, a weary feeling of continually needing to bring people back again to the right path and a despondency that these latest reforms may in the end be no more successful than before, then we may have accurately captured its message. Devotion can be tenuous and short-lived. We must always be on our guard against complacency. The price for staying on track is one of constant vigilance and self-discipline. But as we come to the end of Nehemiah, we know that for us there is more Scripture to enlighten us further, to encourage and uplift us. Above all, we can look to Jesus, the author and perfecter of our faith (Heb. 12:2).

Let's end with the final words that Nehemiah spoke in this book. Appropriately he was speaking to God rather than castigating men, and using once again his favourite word, 'remember'. For Jewish people, remembrance is an integral part of their lives and is a very positive thing. It means to keep something alive by constantly bringing it to the forefront of the mind so that it can be consciously acted upon. As we close the book of Nehemiah, may we always remember it. Let's keep asking what more we can learn from both the man and the message. And let's also keep praying 'Remember me with favour, my God.' Amen!

PART TWO

Topics from the Book of Nehemiah

Introduction

In Part One we have covered the text of the book of Nehemiah in some detail without attempting a full commentary. In doing so we came across certain topics which we said would benefit from a fuller explanation in their own right. This would not only enhance the understanding of these particular passages in Nehemiah but also allow us to develop these themes beyond their initial context in Nehemiah and into our lives today, both as individual Christians and as church communities. That is the aim of Part Two.

The three topics chosen are:

- Enemies and Opposition
- The Book of the Law
- The Feast of Tabernacles

The first of these is very common in Nehemiah, but equally so for us today. How can we relate our experience to that of Nehemiah and the Israelites, and what can we learn from this?

The second is an important topic which Christians are often confused about. What exactly was the Book of the

Law then, and is it relevant for us now? Opinions vary on the role of the Law within Christianity, but once we understand its essential purpose then clarity can emerge and confidence in its application can be gained.

The third is a relatively unknown Jewish feast to Christians (unlike Passover and Pentecost) but one which reveals great depths and insights once its place within God's calendar is recognised.

In each case, more could be said than this book allows, but it is hoped that sufficient is provided here to enable each of us to develop a better understanding and develop our walk with the Lord. If these chapters also encourage further study in these areas, then another aim will also have been fulfilled.

Section 1

Enemies and Opposition

Chapter Sixteen

Overview

In Part One we learnt that Nehemiah faced a great deal of opposition both to himself and to the task of rebuilding the wall of Jerusalem. You can hardly miss it. It is such a regular occurrence throughout the whole book. Danger and difficulties were a constant part of Nehemiah's life from the moment he arrived in Jerusalem. This was all very different from his more comfortable life as cupbearer to King Artaxerxes in the royal palace at Susa.

If Nehemiah was to successfully complete the mission that God had entrusted to him he would have come to terms with everything his enemies could throw at him. He would initially have to understand the nature of the opposition and its purpose. He would also have to learn how to resist the enemy's intentions and then how to combat them in appropriate ways.

We cannot expect anything less by way of opposition to our walk with the Lord and our work for him. So like Nehemiah we need to recognise what we are up against and learn how to withstand the enemy's tactics and overall strategy. Here, in these four short chapters, we cannot provide a comprehensive account of this whole topic but will hopefully be able to offer some key pointers towards a greater understanding of what we face and some vital truths to help us assess the dangers we will encounter.

Let's start by summarising what we find in Nehemiah. There are four main kinds of opposition: personal and corporate, internal and external. Some was personal and individual to Nehemiah; some involved a more corporate attack on the people as a whole. Some came from external enemies, those outside the community of Israel, and still more was brought about by internal strife due to the behaviour of some within the community towards others. There was also ultimately the severe problem of an external enemy becoming internal, someone getting inside not only the community but the very heart of their religious and spiritual life.

More details of all these can be found in Part One of this book as we went through the whole of Nehemiah chapter by chapter, so we will not be repeating everything here. Do go back and read the relevant sections again if you need a refresher, but here is an outline of the main points. Bear in mind that any of these could have derailed the whole building process.

We start in Nehemiah 2:10 where there is the first hint of trouble to come. Certain people, namely Sanballat the Horonite and Tobiah the Ammonite, but no doubt others also, were disturbed that someone (Nehemiah) was coming to Jerusalem to 'promote the welfare of the Israelites'. At this point, no indication is given of how this might play out but clearly the thought that the Israelites might become better protected and generally have more prosperous and peaceful lives was disturbing to many. They were happy while God's people were passive and kept in check, existing but in 'great trouble and disgrace' (1:3, 2:17). We will come back to this important point later.

In Nehemiah 2:19, Sanballat and Tobiah are now joined by Geshem the Arab, or Arabian, and together they begin a campaign of mocking and ridicule. This seems quite gentle at this point, just some mild questions without much force behind them. However, words do have the power to hurt and disrupt. In this case there is a subtle hint that Nehemiah has an ulterior motive, namely to start a rebellion against King Artaxerxes. That's his real motivation, they imply. That's why he's come here. There's a hidden reason behind everything he is planning to do.

Suggesting an ulterior motive is a very powerful way of trying to undermine someone. It creates doubt in the minds of others, and erodes confidence in general. This is especially effective when people are mentally preparing themselves for a new and demanding task. In addition, the fact that Nehemiah had been close to the king, and was presumably still in his service (he doesn't seem to have resigned before leaving Susa), makes him seem even more disloyal and plants a greater sense of treachery in people's minds. Here is someone who has used his position in court to get what he wanted and now he will turn this to his own advantage. Can you trust him as your leader? In the end, won't he abandon you also to suit his own ambitions?

There is a lot behind these few simple words, 'Are you rebelling against the king?' And the intended accusation is no less effective by being framed in the form of a question. It remains highly provocative and could potentially escalate into something more unpleasant. So what is the reaction in this case?

Nehemiah's response is interesting. He doesn't directly tackle the issue of rebellion. He simply expresses faith in God. We are his servants, so he will grant us success. He also adds some facts based upon their history, something we mentioned in more detail in an earlier chapter. His accusers are not part of the people of God so they should leave his work in the hands of those who are.

Was this a wise response? Perhaps Nehemiah should have countered the allegation of rebellion more forcefully, showing them the letters of support from the king, for instance. This might have prevented this kind of attack from re-emerging later. But perhaps he realised there was nothing new in this sort of accusation and it would never totally go away. We saw earlier in this book (Chapter Fifteen) that in Ezra chapter 4, Israel's previous enemies had successfully used these same tactics to halt God's work, so maybe Nehemiah thought the correct approach was not to argue but simply get on with the job and let God deal with the matter.

Christians today will also need to think carefully about the right response to opposition of this kind. We are likely to face such accusations more and more if we maintain traditional Christian standards. Our beliefs and values will put us increasingly at odds with an anti-Christian culture dominated by unbiblical viewpoints and ungodly practices, all backed up with laws intended to enforce compliance. In such circumstances, we could easily be seen as rebelling against society and the authority contained within it. What would our answer be?

When we move to the opening of Nehemiah chapter 4 we find more of the same but with an even greater intensity now that the wall was actually being rebuilt. The initial taunts have failed to demoralise Nehemiah or the people, so further ridicule is now piled up in rapid succession in an attempt to make the Israelites think that what they are doing is all a waste of time. But surely, if their enemies really believed it would all end in failure, in a dismal collapse, why were they so incensed at what was happening? And why go to all the trouble to repeatedly ridicule them in such a vociferous manner? Why didn't they just sit back with a smirk on their faces and watch it all come to nothing?

This level of opposition should be seen in a positive light. It's a sign that you are doing the right thing and that the enemy is getting worried. If persecution increases, take heart. You must be doing something that's pleasing God. If our enemies leave us alone, if they appear apathetic, then that is the time to question if we are really building the kingdom, or anything that will last. So if you have to endure an excess of taunts and ridicule, fear not, pray as Nehemiah did, and carry on!

However, this does not mean things will necessarily get easier. By carrying on, the wall reached half height and the gaps were being closed, so now Israel's enemies stopped firing off insults and started talking to each other, discussing what they might actually do about all this. The result was a plot to inflict physical trouble, perhaps even death. This was now serious, not just because of the possibility of actual bodily harm, but because of the psychological effect. These threats could not easily be dismissed, especially as they were repeatedly made. In the face of such opposition, it is natural for fear to steadily increase and for strength of purpose to flag and even fail.

The response here is twofold. Nehemiah organised a sensible practical plan to ensure such attacks would be minimised, perhaps even deterred completely. But as well as physical preparations for self-defence, Nehemiah also brought truth to the fight. The Lord is great and awesome. Our God will fight for us. We, too, can find many biblical truths to aid us when under attack. Remember, if he is for us, who can be against us? Never forget, God always wins in the end.

The problems recorded in Nehemiah chapter 5 are ones of internal strife and disunity, favourite tactics of our enemy who loves to exploit our fleshly desires at the expense of each other. Brother against brother brings him great satisfaction. We explored earlier, in Chapter Seven, the particular instances that Nehemiah faced, and so we won't repeat all this here, but we can stress again that Nehemiah tackled these with vigour and determination, as indeed must we.

By Nehemiah chapter 6 the wall was built to its full height and all the gaps were closed. You might think Nehemiah could relax at this point, but in fact he now came under even stronger personal attack. Sanballat and Geshem in particular were determined to take revenge. They schemed with the full intention of harming Nehemiah, even killing him. Without discernment, insight, strength of mind and prayer, Nehemiah may well have disappeared from the pages of scripture at this point. The personal attacks upon him were relentless and the dominant weapon used was deception. Lies abounded, whether in the written form of a letter full of fake news and reports or in the spoken messages of false prophets hired to lure him to his death.

These attacks were all intended to intimidate Nehemiah as well as frighten and discourage the people as they saw their leader crumble and fall. But the main tactic of the enemy was to make Nehemiah sin and so diminish or even destroy his relationship with God.

We also see in this chapter of Nehemiah how the allegation of rebellion reappears, this time put more strongly, that Nehemiah was actually conspiring to become king himself. This is why we wondered earlier if Nehemiah could have squashed this accusation better when it first arose. Nevertheless, he was now wise enough to recognise what his enemies were doing. He had developed an awareness of their methods and was better able to protect himself. We, too, can become more mindful of how our enemy operates and develop our defences so that like Nehemiah we are not fooled and can continue the task God has given us.

We have seen before that Nehemiah chapter 13 is full of issues based upon neglect of the house of God, again something the enemy loves to promote, including today where this means neglecting each other as the family of God. But the standout issue was that the enemy in the form of Tobiah had actually got inside the house of God, wrecking the normal running of the religious life of the nation.

How did this come about? Complacency? Compromise? Deception? He's got a good name – Tobiah, that's Jewish, isn't it? He must be one of us really. And he's well connected with the nobles of Judah and through various marriages. Perhaps deep down he's harmless after all or at least deserves a second chance. But it is when we no longer think the enemy is all that dangerous, and let our guard down, that such infiltration occurs. By the time we realise what has happened, it's too late and the damage is done.

Overall we have seen that opposition is manifold, including discouragement, deception, danger, and even death. It may start small, but can build up over time and become more serious. All these aspects of enemy activity are still around and can affect us today, as individuals or as a community. They creep in stealthily, or hit hard suddenly. We need to spot them early and prepare ourselves in advance, strengthening both ourselves and then each other.

Let's end by returning to that statement, in Nehemiah 2:10, that their enemies were disturbed that 'someone had come to promote the welfare of the Israelites'. There are three points here.

Firstly, 'someone'. Not Nehemiah as such but someone, anyone at all. Nehemiah was not important in himself until he began this work for God. Then he came under attack. Previously he was not known to Israel's enemies. Nehemiah the cupbearer to Artaxerxes was of no concern to them, but now he was 'someone' on a mission and this was disturbing. Remaining anonymous is the safe option, but is this really what God is calling us to be?

Secondly, he 'had come', and in particular to Jerusalem. Nehemiah did not face any opposition in Susa, but once he arrived in God's city the attacks began. If you want to avoid enemy opposition, then stay at home. Be comfortable. Stick to your routine. Don't get involved in God's work. Nehemiah could have done this. Instead he went to Jerusalem.

Thirdly, 'the welfare of God's people'. Anyone who promotes the welfare of God's people will face enemy opposition.

This is something the enemy hates, and so too will many who want to live in a secular society run along atheistic principles. We should expect this. Moreover, promoting the welfare of God's people still includes the Jewish people today, who remain the apple of God's eye. Our enemy is also their enemy and he does not like it (nor, incidentally, do many people) when their welfare is promoted in any way. Anti-Jewish feeling is increasingly common, even within Christian communities. Perhaps if Nehemiah had gone anywhere but Jerusalem, the attacks upon him would have been less fierce. But that is where God needed him, and we must be obedient to whatever God wants, regardless of the consequences.

This brief overview has hopefully got us thinking again about this important topic of enemies and opposition, and we will continue to explore this in more depth in our next few chapters.

Chapter Seventeen

Watchmen and Gatekeepers

In the previous chapter we looked briefly through all the different kinds of enemy activity that Nehemiah and the Israelites faced, simply because of Nehemiah's decision to come to Jerusalem and rebuild its broken wall. From this we recognised that anyone who follows God's will and does God's work can expect similar opposition. But from Nehemiah's experiences we can also learn a lot about the enemy's tactics and possible ways of countering these.

Even after the wall had been rebuilt in record time, the dangers were not over. Internal problems re-emerged within the community and one of their enemies from earlier had now gained a serious foothold in the life of the Temple. The constant need to keep a careful watch and take precautions where required was essential if life within the city was to thrive and be pleasing to God.

The same applies to us too. Our stones may be people, living stones, and for us the house of God is the community of Christian believers. But if we are to fit together properly and remain strong then we will need healthy relationships and a spiritual life free from enemy influences and interference. So what kind of protection do we need? What safeguards should we put in place? Let's learn from what Nehemiah did once the building project was completed.

After the wall had been rebuilt and the doors set in place, Nehemiah appointed people to certain roles, two of which are described as guards and gatekeepers (Neh. 7:1-3). This was obviously seen as a critical next step, but why?

On the face of it, this might seem to be nothing more than asking people to keep an eye on things, but there was a lot more to these roles, especially in the case of gatekeepers. It is impossible to understate the crucial nature of the gates of a city. A city obviously needs gates otherwise it is just a prison. As such, gates are the only gaps in a wall that are allowed. But that makes them danger points and so they cannot be left unmonitored. Who or what is permitted to go through the gates determines both the success and safety of a city. Gatekeepers are therefore essential, but before we examine this in detail, let's look first at the other role that Nehemiah insisted on, namely that residents within the city should take on the responsibility of guard duty. We could think of these people as being watchmen. What might a watchman of the wall be expected to do?

Two things come to mind. The first is to be on the lookout for approaching enemies. For this, they might have to go up on top of the wall and scan the horizon for anyone who might be coming to do them harm. A key element of such an attack is surprise, and their enemies could come from almost any direction. So if they didn't want to be caught out then everybody needed to stay alert and be a watchman wherever they were appointed to be.

A second task would be to keep an eye on the wall itself. Are there any loose stones or cracks appearing? Is some repair needed? After all, walls don't look after themselves. They need maintenance if they are to remain strong and it is not a good idea to wait until the enemy is nearby and then do a quick patch up job in the hope that will be sufficient.

So who did Nehemiah appoint to be watchmen of the walls? Who qualified for this role? Everyone! These were ordinary residents of the city. They had all taken part in the rebuilding, so they can all help in keeping it strong. In some cases, they were to watch over the part of the wall near their own homes. You built this bit, so now look after it.

When it comes to our role as watchmen within a Christian community, the same principles apply. We are both those who form the wall, as living stones, but also those who must look after it. This means looking after each other. Is anyone becoming cracked, loose or even detached? That might sound a bit dramatic but people's lives do fall apart at times, and members can suddenly be absent for a while, or go missing entirely. The role of the watchman here is simply to keep asking questions such as 'How are you doing?' or 'How's things going?' or maybe to show concern by commenting that 'We haven't seen you around recently' or 'You're looking tired or stressed, is everything OK?'

The other aspect of watching over people is to see if they are specifically coming under the attack of the enemy at any particular time. Details on this will be considered in a later chapter. But we should always remember that before we can look after others in this respect we have to maintain our own personal defences. That is our primary responsibility. Only then can we be strong enough to be of service to others.

In summary, as watchmen (and women!) we should be strengthening and repairing each other where necessary but also warning one another of dangers that are all around. People do get tempted and go astray. It is easy to get complacent at times. We should all watch for such signs and be prepared to ask, 'Should you be doing that? Going there? Talking like that?'

We have to take this seriously. As someone once commented to me, a reluctance to challenge each other makes us vulnerable to the enemy's attack. That's a powerful and wise statement, and it's worth repeating. Reluctance to challenge each other makes us more vulnerable to the attacks of our enemy.

Those who travel on the London Underground are likely to hear a recorded message exhorting people to keep an eye out for anything suspicious and report it. The various ways of doing this are then announced, followed by the memorable slogan 'See it. Say it. Sorted.' The implication being that just seeing it is not enough. Without saying something, it won't get sorted.

Who are to be our watchmen? As in Nehemiah, all of us. Everyone can take part in looking after each other. One person cannot look after everyone, but if everyone looks after someone then our whole 'wall' will be protected in this way. It is not just the job of the church leader, or the elders, or leaders of small groups. We are all watchmen, guardians of our precious people.

Of course, there is the other side of this too. Do we want to be watched over? We might regard the questions mentioned above as interfering or intrusive. We would rather remain private and not open up our lives to others in this way. This in turn might create a reluctance to challenge people in case they get annoyed or offended. So for all this to work, being looked after by each other has to be welcomed, even invited, and become part of the culture of the church community. If occasionally this goes a bit wrong or is overdone, then let forgiveness do its work. Then let's learn to do this better, rather than give up.

Let's remember how James ends his letter. 'My brothers and sisters, if one of you should wander from the truth and someone should bring that person back, remember this: whoever turns a sinner from the error of their way will save them from death and cover over a multitude of sins' (James 5:19-20). Any one of us could wander. It happens. And anyone could bring us back. James just says 'someone', not necessarily a leader. It could be one of your closest friends, someone who knows you well. But it might just be anyone. Anyone who cares enough, that is.

What about gatekeepers? They are more specific and more specialist. This is not for everyone, at least not automatically. They need to be carefully chosen. Nehemiah appointed 172 such men (Neh. 11:19). Originally at the time of the first return, there were 138 who were designated as gatekeepers (Neh. 7:45), but it appears that now the gates were actually in place again, Nehemiah decided more were needed. 172 may seem a lot for about a dozen gates, but obviously there wasn't just one keeper per gate, or even two or three. They worked in large teams and presumably in shifts too. Overall, the total number was about 4 or 5 per cent of the city's population.

City gates were not, of course, like the front door to your house or the gates to your driveway. They were massive and needed to be very thick. They were also very heavy, as the wood was usually strengthened with sheets of metal such as iron or brass, so it took more than just a couple of men to open and close each one. For example, it is said that the Beautiful Gate of Herod's Temple mentioned in Acts 3:2 required twenty men to shut it and secure it.

As an interesting comparison we read in 1 Chronicles 26 about the doorkeepers of the Temple. There seems to be over 200 of these in total. The details are worth noting (1 Chron. 26:17-18). Each day six Levites guarded the east gate, with four on each of the north and south gates. As for the west, there were four on the road (presumably just outside the gate) and two at the court. In addition, there were two at a time at the storehouse. Perhaps most significant is the statement that 'Guard was alongside guard' (1 Chron. 26:16). This was not to be a solitary occupation. Again we see teams at work, with all points covered. Clearly this was an important duty and had to be taken seriously.

As we have already said, gates were essential points of entry and exit, and therefore places where the city was most vulnerable. But they were also significant because of the many activities that took place at or near the gates. You may recall some of these from certain Old Testament passages.

The gates represented places of judgement and authority, where justice was administered and where citizens could take their complaints and grievances. The elders of a city sat at the gates to give rulings and make wise decisions which would hopefully resolve all such disputes. Perhaps that's why Proverbs 1:21 says that it is at the gateways of the city that wisdom makes her speeches.

Prophets also would proclaim their messages at the gates knowing there would be a ready audience there. Jeremiah was specifically told by God on one occasion to do this not just at one gate but at all the gates of Jerusalem as this would maximise the impact of the word of the Lord (Jer. 17:19-20).

Important meetings took place at city gates. In one case, the kings of Israel and Judah met at the gate of Samaria to discuss attacking the Arameans (see 1 Kgs 22:10ff, 2 Chron. 18:9ff). Business transactions and contracts were often made and witnessed by city elders at the gates, a good example being that of Boaz in Ruth chapter 4. Ruth's father and husband were both dead, so Boaz sat down at the city gate to discuss Ruth's inheritance with her nearest relative, the so-called kinsman-redeemer. Ten of the town elders joined them and witnessed the discussion and the eventual agreement that Boaz would marry Ruth and buy the family land in order to maintain her father's name and property.

So what was expected of a city gatekeeper? As with the watchmen and the walls, one aspect would be to check if repairs were needed. Was the wood still strong enough? Did the hinges work properly? Would the gate close securely? But gatekeepers were also charged with opening and closing the gates at the right time. These times were set in advance and not allowed to vary. Citizens needed to know exactly when they could come and go, and trust that the gates would be closed and barred at dusk for their safety (see Josh. 2:5-7 as an example). Residents had a right to expect that all this would be done properly, and that the gatekeepers could be relied upon to spot any dangers and protect them accordingly. Was anyone prowling around outside at night, for instance? In addition, gatekeepers had to be ready to shut the gates at a moment's notice if needed, and to stay strong in the face of enemies at the gates.

We have seen in the past that Nehemiah had ordered the gates of Jerusalem to be kept shut until midday each day and that no traders should be allowed in on the Sabbath. So when he returned to Jerusalem and discovered this had not happened, he was very angry and took action. He replaced the gatekeepers responsible and appointed others instead, those he could rely on (Neh. 13:19-22).

There is much here that applies to us. A church also has its own kind of gates, contact points with the outside world. These cannot be permanently closed. We have to engage with the world, not stay within holy huddles. But dangers are waiting every time we go outside the protection of our 'wall'. Also, by necessity a Christian community itself has to be a gateway so others can find entry into the kingdom of God. But again, our enemy is always just outside, waiting like Tobiah to sneak in and bring disruption. It is a tricky balance. We have to be welcoming but wise. We will discuss some of these dangers in a later chapter.

Another comparison is in the critical area of making decisions and judgments, resolving complaints and disputes. Those with wisdom and maturity need to sit at these particular gates in order to keep the Christian community healthy and free from hostility, as this is another way in which the enemy creeps into our spiritual lives and creates disorder and disarray.

Every member of a Christian community should be confident that gatekeepers are in place to provide them with the necessary protection in all these ways. Vigilance and diligence are needed if the house of God is not to be neglected. Being a gatekeeper is therefore an awesome responsibility, and, as we have said earlier, not for everyone. So what makes a good gatekeeper? Who is best qualified for this role? Quite simply, those who guard their own personal gates, which will be the focus of our next chapter.

Chapter Eighteen

Personal Gates

In the previous chapter we have explained about the importance of gates within a city wall, and hence the vital role of gatekeepers. We then saw how a church or Christian community has its own form of gates, contact points with the outside world, and that these also need protecting from the enemy waiting to sneak in, or even force his way inside. Clearly, then, a church needs its own gatekeepers as well, so we ended the previous chapter by asking who would make good gatekeepers, who is best qualified for this role? The answer, or at least part of it, is those who guard their own personal gates. So what does this mean? What are our personal gates?

John Bunyan is well known for one book, *The Pilgrim's Progress*, but he did write others, including one called *The Holy War*. This book, like *The Pilgrim's Progress*, is also an allegory, and describes the battle between Shaddai (God) and Diabolus. This battle is centred on Mansoul, a town founded and built by Shaddai for his own delight and glory. Mansoul was intended for its maker alone, but another (Shaddai's enemy, Diabolus) has laid siege to it in order to take it for himself. The walls of this human city are well built but contain five gates, described by Bunyan as the Ear-gate, Eye-gate, Mouth-gate, Nose-gate and Feel-gate.

In this way Bunyan takes our five senses and depicts them as personal gates or contact points with the world around us. Obviously, these senses are necessary gateways for us, otherwise we could not live properly in our world, but, just as in a city, they also create danger areas, places of greatest threat. Collectively they convey the outside world into the mind and from there feed into a man's soul. So, not surprisingly, it is outside these gates that the enemy is encamped, waiting to bring harm and corruption into a human life.

A lot of this should be very obvious to us. Perhaps the Nose-gate may not seem to offer much of a threat (though what we inhale can be damaging!) but we are surely aware that what we see and hear impacts us greatly. What we touch can also have an influence upon us, so we do need to be careful how we use our hands and what we allow them to do. Our Mouth-gate is another vital point of entry and exit. What we take in through our mouth is significant but, as Jesus made clear, it is primarily what comes *out* of a man's mouth that makes him unclean (Matt. 15:11). James in his letter adds that the tongue can corrupt the whole person. He describes it as a restless evil, full of deadly poison, which no man can tame (see James chapter 3). We must watch what we say, or, to put it another way, we must guard our tongue.

We could add another gate to Bunyan's list, the Feet-gate, for where our feet take us can put us in places which allow the enemy further opportunities to attack our 'mansoul' through other gates. We need to guard where we go.

And then there is our heart. Much of what we have been saying could be encapsulated by the call to guard our heart at all times. Proverbs 4:23 warns of the need for this: 'Above all else', it reads, 'guard your heart, for everything you do flows from it.' This wise advice is followed in verses 24-27 by similar counsel about our mouth, eyes and feet. These few verses from Proverbs chapter 4 are worth storing away for further contemplation when the need arises.

Overall, this theme of guarding our personal gates will run through much of what we have to say in this chapter and the one that follows. But let's explore next what our enemy is like, and check out some of his tactics.

It is often said we have three adversaries: the world, the flesh, and the devil. This is not a phrase that can be found in the Bible in so many words (it first appears within the 1544 Litany, later incorporated into the *Book of Common Prayer*, 1662), but it does sum up much of what the Bible teaches in this regard. However, it might be better to say there is really only one enemy, the devil, with the other two (the world and the flesh) being his main methods of attack or the chief weapons in his armoury. Clearly, these three are interrelated with an immense collective power, but we can also examine them separately, which we now do briefly in order to understand the essence of each.

Let's start with the flesh. Although the Greek word (*sarx*) can refer to our physical body, this is not its main meaning in the Bible. There is nothing wrong as such with the material part of us, our fleshly bodies. The problem is the sinful nature within as described in Ephesians 2:3, with its cravings, desires and capacity to create lustful thoughts, all generally summed up as carnal ways.

The point is that our passions and appetites may feel natural to the body but in reality can in some cases be the very opposite of what God desires for us. They may 'feel right' but in effect are corrupt versions of what God intends, even acts of rebellion against him. In this sense, the word 'flesh' refers to how our human nature opposes God and his ways, causing us instead to chase after self-gratification and self-enhancement. As such the flesh is a very dangerous enemy, or, if you prefer, a very powerful weapon in the hand of our chief enemy.

Moreover, this biblical concept of the flesh relates not just to the body but also to the mind, which equally has its own cravings as it seeks new ideas, the latest fashions, and whatever else we believe will lead to our self-improvement. This can also spill over into our spiritual life as we may wonder if there is a version of Christianity that might serve us better, or which could be more satisfying to us and our needs. Perhaps we can update Christianity (after all, the Bible is rather old-fashioned), or make it more acceptable to those who have rejected the traditional version? Maybe we ought to listen to what those in the world would prefer, and be adaptable to their wishes?

All this comes under the idea of 'the flesh', the way we let our inner desires, either individually or collectively as humanity, draw us away from God. The flesh puts man on the throne of life, and tells us that the only true god worth serving and worshipping is the self. Once this attitude is installed, then seductive paths are created and easy to follow. Our gates will be breached.

So what kind of gatekeeper is needed here? What can be done? Contrary to popular modern opinion the inner self must be controlled and denied, not indulged or accommodated in any way. Allowing the self to reign unchecked simply causes the problem to grow and the flesh to become more animalistic or carnal. The Bible is clear. The flesh cannot be entertained or allowed for. It has to be crucified (see Gal. 5:24, Rom. 8:13). This may sound brutal and painful but unless we put the flesh to death it will always fight back.

Simply trying to manage the impact of the flesh or keep it in check will never succeed. You have to launch a militant campaign against it. The Bible tells us we do this 'by the Spirit' (see Rom. 8:13 again). We must not sow to the flesh by feeding it what it wants, but sow to the Spirit, which means constantly walking in the Spirit, or keeping in step with the Spirit. Willpower is usually not enough. It may be sufficient when it comes to denying yourself too much chocolate, for instance, but by itself this will not overcome stronger addictions or the more potent attractions of fleshly desires. We need the power of the Holy Spirit firmly at work in our lives. This is the only way to shut this gate, and to guard it.

Let's turn next to 'the world'. Again, the Greek word (*kosmos*) can have several meanings. It can refer to the whole universe (the cosmos) or the planet on which we live. God created all this, so that is not our enemy. The word can also refer to everyone who lives in the world, as in John 3:16, which tells us how much God loved the world by sending his Son to die for all people. Again this meaning of *kosmos* is positive. People as such are not our enemy, though they may give a good impression of one at times! But as Ephesians 6:12 explains, this is not where our main struggle lies. Rather, our battle is against the powers of this dark world and the spiritual forces of evil which inhabit the heavenly realms.

The real enemy which we call 'the world' is a system, a system of practices and standards which are primarily anti-God. As such it is more than just ungodly, it is godless. It operates with man in charge without God in his thinking at all. It feeds on the pride of humanity and develops as people give in to fleshly ways and carnal thinking. Thus the twin forces of the world and the flesh are linked, reinforcing each other in a powerful way.

This is more than a social or political system. It is an atmosphere, a pollutant we breathe in every day and which then circulates in our collective bloodstream. It invades everything and is designed to eliminate God's rule and presence, setting up false and blasphemous alternatives.

We talk of worldly ways or worldliness. By this we mean the network of ideas, values, morals, practices and norms that are integrated into the mainstream of life and institutionalised in a culture corrupted by the redefinition of good and evil. The distorted becomes normative and sets up its own wisdom, a wisdom that is not from God but that is earthly, unspiritual, of the devil (Jas 3:15).

This brings us neatly to our third or main enemy, the devil. There is much that could be said here, and in our next chapter we will focus on how he operates, but for now let us consider a title that he is given.

Three times in John's Gospel Jesus refers to him as the *prince* or *ruler* of this world (John 12:31, 14:30, 16:11). In Greek the word for ruler is *archon*, commonly used within the Roman world in New Testament times for the highest-ranking Roman official in a city or region, effectively the most powerful and influential person in that particular locality. So by calling him the *archon* of the cosmos, Jesus is emphasising not just the magnitude of the devil's power and influence but also its extent. It stretches beyond one place into all the kingdoms of this world. No-one can escape his reach or control. Moreover, he has held sway in the whole world throughout its entire existence, and has been instrumental in how human thought and activity has developed over time in every area of life.

In Ephesians 2:2 Paul also uses *archon* when describing the devil. Here, Paul calls him 'the ruler of the kingdom of the air', another way of referring to his influence over the whole world. Incidentally, in 2 Corinthians 4:4 Paul calls him the god (*theos*) of this age, reflecting how men have allowed the enemy to take God's place in human affairs throughout history as well as in their individual lives.

It is the extent of our enemy's rule over the earthly kingdoms of this world which makes this such a powerful weapon, and a threat to us. It's also why the devil could tempt Jesus with the gift of these kingdoms in return for worship (Matt. 4:8-9). Jesus resisted this and so must we. We are chosen to be 'not of this world' otherwise we become easy prey to its ruler. We also note that Jesus pronounced judgement upon the world and its prince (see John 12:31, 16:11). In addition, he issued a stern warning by asking, 'What good is it for someone to gain the whole world, yet forfeit their soul?' (Mark 8:36). It is that serious.

We have already shown how we all have personal gates that the enemy can and will attack. He is constantly looking for unprotected gates in order to gain access into our life. These days we are increasingly subject to vast amounts of input from so many sources on a daily basis. We need to be fully aware of the effect of what we see, hear, speak about and think of, as well as our choices of where we go and whom we spend time with. We must actively identify where we are most vulnerable, not just in terms of how we feed our fleshly desires but also the beliefs we operate in, the decisions we make and our general perception of the world around us. It only takes one gate to be unguarded to allow our enemy to gain a foothold, and once a gate is conquered, he then places his own gatekeepers there, to keep it open for further invasion and to make it more difficult for us to close it again. We should also remember that gates are places of authority. If we do not submit them to God's authority, then they will be more easily captured by the world, the flesh or the devil.

We end this chapter with something from Paul. In Ephesians 6:11 he exhorts us to take a stand against the devil's schemes, sometimes translated as his wiles or devices. The Greek word is *methodeias*, suggesting methods, that which is predictable, well known and often used. The good news is that the devil has no new tactics or weapons. The bad news: he doesn't need any. The old ones still work very well. But this means we can and should become familiar with his methods. Paul states in 2 Corinthians 2:11, 'we are not unaware of his schemes'. Our defence starts with awareness, then we can begin to protect ourselves further. In Ephesians 6:13-18 Paul tells us to take our stand against the devil's schemes by putting on the full armour of God. God has provided so much to help us here. Take a look sometime at these verses and the items mentioned, and notice how they relate to our gates. There is a helmet to cover our head, a breastplate for our heart, a shield and sword for our hands, shoes on our feet, and a belt of truth around our waist. This last item is particularly important if we are to counter the devil's main weapon, namely lies. This is the subject of our next chapter.

Chapter Nineteen

The Enemy and His Lies

In this section we have already seen the importance of gates and gatekeepers, for ourselves as individuals as well as for a church or Christian community. Our enemy is always poised at these gates ready to attack through the twin weapons of the world and the flesh, and we ended last time by saying that his main tactic is that of lies, which is the subject of this chapter.

Jesus tells us that the devil is the father of lies, and that when he lies he speaks his native language (John 8:44). He is the origin of all that is fake and false in our world. From the beginning he has never stopped telling lies. He generates them, plants them and nurtures them, watching over them until they change lives, societies and even nations. Every society on earth is now full of his weeds of deception and untruth, so much so that these are seen as normal. They have become the common currency of our fallen world and explain much of what goes on in it. We should realise that in essence our battle against the world, the flesh and the devil is one against lies. They come from the devil, feed into the flesh, and from there are normalised into the world.

Jesus' words in John 8:44 warn us that the devil communicates his lies by speaking, something which we also find in Genesis chapter 3 at the time of the first temptation and deception. How he speaks can vary. It may be through actual words, spoken by human voices and heard out loud. Or it may be voices in the head, whispers in the ear, impressions or thoughts in the mind. All these are attacks on the Ear-gate. When Jesus was tempted in the wilderness he heard words. We may not know exactly how this occurred but words were used, and countered by Jesus speaking back from the written Word of God.

Watch out for when the devil speaks. By his very nature, this must be a lie of some kind. There is an old joke sometimes used against people. 'How do you know he's lying? It's easy. His lips are moving!' A bit cruel, perhaps; no-one is that bad. But very true when it comes to the devil.

But lies are not just spoken; they are lived. And these are the worst kind. What may start with being heard is then believed and ultimately lived out. The lie becomes part of a mindset or worldview and then part of a lifestyle. Lies that are lived are most dangerous because they are seen by others. They attack the Eye-gate. And what we see can become what we want. We tend to believe what we see and then decide it must be all right. It seems fun or normal, so we want this too, and will change in order to live that way. This is another part of our enemy's clever strategy.

In the Garden of Eden, Eve didn't just hear what the serpent said, she could also see the fruit of the forbidden tree. But once the serpent had talked to her, she saw it in a different way. It had now become 'good' and 'pleasing to the eye' (Gen. 3:6). I suspect that the serpent was clever enough to talk to her within sight of that tree. He probably waited until she was close enough to the tree to be able to see it before engaging in conversation. 'We can't eat from the tree in the middle of the garden.' 'Oh, you mean that one, over there?'

All very subtle. Our enemy will always direct our eyes as well as whisper in our ears, knowing that this will create new desires or intensify existing ones.

'We can't steal from a shop.' 'You mean like that one over there, with lots of nice things in the window that you can't afford?'

'We can't have sex with anyone we are not married to.' 'You mean like that attractive person whom you see every day at work or next door?'

A dual attack on our Ear-gate and Eye-gate is very powerful. You need your best gatekeepers guarding these entrances to your life and soul.

Another tactic of our lying enemy is the half-truth. What's the problem with a half-truth? The other half. It is the truthful bit which makes it appealing. An out-and-out lie can appear ridiculous, totally unbelievable. But if part of it is true, then this carries the rest into our minds where it can settle and affect us.

The bit that is true can be more than half, indeed much more, but there is still enough of a lie to be dangerous. For instance, how poisonous is rat poison? Very, might be a good answer. But, in fact, over 99.99 per cent is good stuff – what rats like and will readily eat. Just 0.0025 per cent (that's 1 part in 40,000) is poison. So how poisonous is rat poison? Hardly at all. Or 100 per cent deadly, depending on your point of view. 'Just one feed is all you need' would be a good advertising slogan.

Christians are just as susceptible to half-truths as anyone else. New phrases and ideas which seem appealing or desirable remain unchecked against biblical truth, and then get passed on within the Christian world. They get accepted, repeated, and eventually assumed to be true, almost beyond criticism. They may even become embedded within a particular theology though they don't represent God in any way, either his will, his feelings or his revealed plans.

One half-truth that is repeatedly told and commonly accepted in the world at large is that humanity is continually improving, getting better and better with each succeeding generation. C.S. Lewis called this idea 'chronological snobbery', the view that we are automatically smarter and more advanced than our parents. On the face of it, this seems true. Evidence suggests that the average IQ has been increasing recently and knowledge is clearly growing all the time. But is knowledge alone a good measure of human advancement? Moreover, just because *some* things have improved (medicine, travel, communication, and so on) it is false to imply that *everything* is now so much better. This is one way deception can work. Take one particular thing that is obviously true and then extend it to everything. People will accept the former, and hence believe the generalisation even if it is not true overall. In this way they can be led astray.

Of course, few would want to go back and live in previous centuries. The many benefits of our modern age have enhanced life, but they have also created a belief in progress which has blinded us, or at least blurred our vision of what is true and false. We now trust our new ideas rather than revelation from the past which is seen as outdated, maybe fine for people then but not for us now.

The argument seems compelling. We know so much more today in many areas of life, so we must now be clever enough to know better than our ancestors in every way. We use phrases like 'in this day and age' and 'we can't believe that nowadays' to emphasise the point. And because we are more advanced today, we are told we can forget about the superstitious nonsense of the past, such as the existence of the devil himself. And this is his biggest triumph: to persuade us that he doesn't exist! There's no need to flee the devil if he isn't there!

Another point to bear in mind is that in both Greek and Hebrew the word for 'true' is also the word for 'real'. What is true is real. So reality can only be based upon what is true and will not adjust itself to wrong ideas and false beliefs. There can be nothing real about a lie. Lies contain false assumptions about reality, so if a lie becomes truth for us, this will drive us into unreality.

We should also understand that the lies of our enemy are not just any old facts that are untrue. For them to reshape our lives they have to get into our hearts. As such they are often loaded with emotional pulling power. Many lies may leave us unmoved, but if we are told that this is what we really deserve, that it will make us happier or ultimately bring more self-satisfaction, then we are more likely to be enticed and drawn in further. After all, our main obligation is always to ourselves, isn't it? We need to watch out for such seductive phrases.

Overall, our enemy is very skilful at making us imagine something is true when it is actually false. Our capacity to believe a lie is astonishing at times. But lies are never neutral. They have consequences which can be deadly. Our gates need to be guarded very securely against all these schemes and, as we saw at the end of the last chapter, for this we need the full armour of God, including the belt of truth firmly fastened around our waist, holding everything together.

But it is not just our personal gates that come under attack in these ways. The enemy can just as easily break through the gates of a church or Christian community, if left unprotected. Let's look briefly at how this can happen.

Jesus warned repeatedly about deception, false teachers and false prophets (see Matthew chapter 24 for instance). Each of these is a huge topic in itself, but for now we will have to be content with providing some signs of what these entail.

One indication that the enemy has infiltrated the gates of a church is that the gospel is no longer preached, or maybe a different gospel is proclaimed which is really no gospel at all (Gal. 1:6-9). There is no mention of sin or guilt, no sense of conviction or need for a Saviour. Instead, the true message of salvation is replaced by a 'feel better' therapeutic gospel, which tells people they are loved but leaves them unchanged and not in a relationship with their heavenly Father through Jesus. Every time the gospel is diluted to make it more appealing, it loses its power, and the enemy has won a crucial victory.

Clearly, teachers are important with a Christian community. Their role is to speak out biblical truth and help people to understand it better. So false teachers are deadly, leading people astray if allowed to continue. But to be clear, just getting something wrong does not make someone a false teacher. We all get things wrong. False teachers are altogether different. They may profess to respect scripture but throw doubt on its teaching. They pursue a different agenda and consistently promote teaching that is contrary to the gospel and the Bible as a whole. This may be subtly done but can be spotted by gatekeepers who know their Bible thoroughly and can test what is taught. Another sign of a false teacher is if they are self-serving or linked to a false theology (more on this in a moment).

False prophets are equally dangerous, especially if also self-serving. Again, this is not a matter of an occasional mistake. Rather a false prophet will regularly promote something that isn't right, consistently contradict scripture or say things that produce no fulfilled outcomes or change. Scriptural examples include proclaiming peace when there is no peace, and calling good evil and evil good (see Isa. 5:20-21; Jer. 6:14, 8:11; Ezek. 13:10-16). On the other hand, a true prophet is someone whose words are never dictated by their natural inclinations. They have a mind that is constantly directed towards God's throne. They have great faith and a strong moral character, plus a broad knowledge of scripture; not necessarily a deep knowledge (teachers provide this) but a breadth that will keep them in line with God's revelation.

As we saw in Nehemiah, the greatest menace can come from within. The presence within a church of a type of faith or practice that is anti-Christian will ruin it and ultimately destroy it. The kind of theology a church embraces is crucial in this respect and there seems to be many alternatives to choose from. New kinds of liberal theology emerge all the time, reacting against traditional orthodoxy which is seen as being too rigid. We must be more flexible. We don't need statements of faith, creeds, or dogmatism. We should adjust to the surrounding culture. The intention may be to rescue Christianity from external loathing or indifference, but a watered-down liberal version of Christianity which accommodates the spirit of the age will only result in a religious form of postmodernism which has surrendered truth and replaced discipleship with a kind of club membership.

Gatekeepers of these particular gates should watch out for terms like 'emerging' or 'emergent' or 'progressive'. They should beware of prosperity teaching which equates material wealth with spiritual blessing, a throwback to the Sadducees of the New Testament. They need to guard against those who profess to be more apostolic than the original apostles or who claim greater prophetic insights than the biblical prophets or those whom God used to write down his Word. These gatekeepers should also be wary of the many end time scenarios that have arisen in recent times based upon human imagination and desire rather than the revelation of scripture. They need to watch for those who scoff at the thought of Christ's return or who espouse teaching which says the church can defeat the devil and all his works before Christ returns, which must have the devil laughing his head off – assuming he exists, that is.

Gatekeepers must especially be alert for one of the most subtle yet prevalent dangers that can infiltrate a Christian community, namely replacement theology, which teaches that God has changed his mind about the Jewish people and replaced them with the church. He has discarded his earlier covenants and broken his promises to the Jewish people. He has effectively 'unchosen' them in favour of the church which has taken their place. Not only does this false teaching tear out great chunks of scripture, which have to be ignored or reinterpreted, it also changes the nature of God and how we should understand him. Yet this huge lie is regularly taught, either directly or by implication.

As for Bible translations, none are perfect but there are some that set out to take us away from truth and traditional teaching. They are designed to support false teachers and false theology, so always check where a new translation comes from and what its purpose is.

It is the same with new songs and choruses. There are so many these days, but where do they come from? What are they really saying? They may be easy to sing, tuneful and rhythmical, but that doesn't mean they are scriptural. Test each line. Errors may be deliberate, to promote false teaching, or unintentional, simply based upon creating a rhyme or fitting the metre, but either way what we sing enters our Ear-gate and goes deeply into us. One line of a song or a few verses or passages in a whole Bible may not seem much, but remember that rat poison!

Being a gatekeeper is demanding. As we've said, it is not for everyone. To be a gatekeeper requires one quality in particular, something Nehemiah had to have, namely discernment. There are two kinds of discernment. One is a special gift, a discernment of spirits. We can confidently ask God for this gift as he always wants to help us. The other is a more general quality that comes with maturity, constantly walking with God and spending time in his Word.

We *can* learn to discern the truth from the lie. We can be trained to distinguish good from evil (see Heb. 5:14).

As we close this section let's take heart from Jesus' prayer for his disciples in John 17:17, when he said, 'Sanctify them by the truth; your word is truth.'

Section 2

The Book of the Law

Chapter Twenty

The Book of the Law of Moses

This new section focuses on a topic that occurs regularly throughout the second half of Nehemiah, from chapter 8 onwards, where it is introduced as 'The Book of the Law of Moses'. In Nehemiah 8:1 Ezra the scribe is told to 'bring out' this book, which we are told is something 'which the LORD had commanded for Israel'.

We didn't have time to explore this in Part One of our book as we wanted to keep going through Nehemiah, so we said we would come back to this later, especially as it inevitably raises certain questions that need careful consideration. Hopefully, we can now provide some answers to these and to the topic of the Law in general as this is often something that Christians are uncertain about or confused over. A wrong understanding here can have far-reaching consequences and adversely affect much within the Christian faith.

The reading of the Book of the Law of Moses is an important part of the later chapters in Nehemiah. The rebuilding of the wall of Jerusalem was now complete and the gates had been set in place. It was now time to rebuild or reform the people, to create a godly society within the city of God. To this end the Law of Moses was crucial and much time was spent reading it and hearing it read.

But what exactly is meant by this phrase 'the Book of the Law of Moses'? Was it actually a book, and what was in it? We also need to ask what this should mean for us today. Do we have this book in some form or other, and if so how should we regard it? Is it relevant or obsolete, only of historical interest?

In Nehemiah we are not told much about its content. In one place we learn that they read about the Feast of Tabernacles (Neh. 8:14), a topic which we will cover later, and in another verse (Neh. 13:1) we see that the Israelites discovered that no Ammonite or Moabite should ever be admitted into the assembly of God. Beyond that there is very little of a clue.

We find that it was often read at great length over many hours; on one occasion for six hours, from daybreak until noon (Neh. 8:3), and on another for three hours, a quarter of the day (Neh. 9:3). It was also read regularly on several separate occasions, often on consecutive days (Neh. 8:13, 18).

We are also told how the people reacted when it was read to them. This varied from praise and worship (Neh. 8:5-6), to weeping (Neh. 8:9), to confession and worship (Neh. 9:3), and to joyful action (Neh. 9:14-17). This latter response was when they learnt that they should be celebrating the Feast of Tabernacles and decided to put this right at once, leading to very great joy.

Let's start by looking at what this book is actually called. In Nehemiah it is described in various ways. In 8:1 it is the

Book of the Law of Moses. In 8:8 and 8:18 it is the Book of the Law of God, and in 9:3 it is called the Book of the Law of the Lord their God. In 8:3 it is just the Book of the Law and in 13:1 it is the Book of Moses. Finally, in 8:9 it is even more succinctly described as the words of the Law.

There is no need to try and distinguish between these. The names may be different, but the actual book is the same in each case. In full, it is the Book of the Law of God (Elohim), their Lord (Adonai) given to them via Moses (Moshe). That's rather a mouthful so shorter versions were clearly used.

Was it actually a book? In all of the above descriptions, the Hebrew word is *sefer*, which is accurately translated as 'book' though in practice this would be a scroll or maybe even more than one scroll. Incidentally, the word *sefer* relates to the idea of reading, so in effect it is anything that can be read. It was also used for their first level of schooling. Aged five, Jewish boys went to their *Beit Sefer* (house of reading), a place where they learnt to read, and in particular to read the sacred texts. They started with the book of Leviticus, perhaps not our first choice but for them it was the most exciting place to begin as this book contains more of the direct words of God than any other. As a young boy, Jesus would have attended a *Beit Sefer* and started his learning with Leviticus.

Today when we hear the phrase the 'Law of Moses' we think of the first five books in our Bible. We often call these the books of Moses or the Pentateuch. We may also have heard it called the Torah, and been told that this means Law. We will be thinking more about this important word in our next chapter as this is where a lot of confusion can arise.

These first five books of the Bible are traditionally ascribed to Moses but that is not the same as saying that he wrote every word of them. The books themselves don't claim he was their author. In fact, they speak of Moses in the third person (rather than as a first-person narrator). However, he may have helped compile them in some way or been responsible for certain parts of them. Scholars have come up with several complicated theories for the final form of the Pentateuch, saying that these books draw on four different strands which contribute towards the whole and which were brought together into a single work at some later date.

There may or may not be some truth in this. Other scholars inevitably disagree with these ideas, such is the nature of the academic world. But for our purposes we can disregard these arguments and accept that what we have today is a unified composition with Moses as the central character (after God, of course) and the potential writer of much of it, at least in its initial form.

However, there are certain portions of the Pentateuch he couldn't possibly have written directly and others which are rather improbable. For instance, Moses doesn't appear in Genesis at all and it is unlikely that he wrote about his own birth and childhood in the opening of Exodus. In the same way, his death in Deuteronomy 34:5-12 must have been recorded by someone else!

There are other bits which indicate later editorial comments or asides by someone else. In Genesis 12:6 we read that 'At that time the Canaanites were in the land'. This is referring to the time of Abraham when the Canaanites certainly did occupy the land through which Abraham travelled. But this verse is implying that at the time of writing the Canaanites were no longer there. However, during the entire life of Moses there were still Canaanites in the land, so this comment only makes sense if it was written by someone else afterwards.

Equally, are we to believe that Moses wrote the comment in Numbers 12:3 which reads, 'Now Moses was a very humble man, more humble than anyone else on the face of the earth'? Moses was the most modest of men, said Moses! Surely someone else penned this as a later epitaph to an extraordinary man.

Now the point of all this is that it is highly unlikely that in Nehemiah, the Book of the Law of Moses refers to the entire collection of writings we now know of as Genesis to Deuteronomy. By my estimate this would take about twelve hours to read straight through without any added explanations, so it is too long to fit into any of the sessions recorded in Nehemiah. In addition, did they need to hear everything contained in these five books at that time? Was this really the main purpose behind reading the Law to everyone there and then?

There is always the possibility that the Book of the Law of Moses refers to just one book, such as Deuteronomy. This is often regarded as a good candidate to be a stand-alone version of the Law. Its name translates as 'second Law', not in the sense of an update or later version, but rather as a summary of all that has gone before but without most of the narrative or 'stories'. The opening of Deuteronomy defines itself as 'These are the words Moses spoke' so this fits the bill. In fact 'These are the words' is its proper name as in the Hebrew Bible books were titled after their opening words, the first ones you saw as you began to unroll the scroll. The title Deuteronomy is a later Greek name for it.

But there is another real possibility, namely that what they read in Nehemiah's time was not anything that we have today, at least not in that same form. It might eventually have become incorporated into one or more of the books of the Pentateuch, but in its time it existed in its own right as a separate document. Is there any evidence for this and if so what would it contain?

There are certain passages in the Pentateuch which suggest that Moses was indeed personally involved in preserving a written copy of the Law that God gave to his people. For example, in Exodus chapter 24 we read that 'When Moses went and told the people all the LORD's words and laws, they responded with one voice, "Everything the LORD has said we will do."' This is Exodus 24:3, and in the following verse it goes on to say, 'Moses then wrote down *everything the LORD had said*' (italics mine).

This is different from saying that Moses actually wrote Exodus chapter 24 itself, but this chapter is telling us that somehow, somewhere, and at some time Moses put into writing all the words and laws of God that he (Moses) had just passed on to the people. Later in this chapter, Exodus 24:7, this is referred to as the Book of the Covenant. It was this which was read to the people who responded by saying they would obey everything in it, a typically enthusiastic response at the time and one we also find in the book of Nehemiah. Was it therefore perhaps this that was read to the people of God then?

We find this sort of thing again in Deuteronomy chapter 31. It is worth reading this chapter carefully. In Deuteronomy

31:9 it says, 'So Moses wrote down this law and gave it to the Levitical priests, who carried the ark of the covenant of the LORD, and to all the elders of Israel.' This was the Law that was to be read before the people in their hearing. In addition, verse 24 of the same chapter adds that shortly before his death Moses 'finished writing in a book the words of this law from beginning to end'. Incidentally, we also find in verses 19 and 22 that Moses wrote down the words of the song which we have in the next chapter of Deuteronomy, chapter 32.

Overall, verses like this indicate that Moses did indeed write down parts of what we have as scripture, but perhaps only the words that he heard directly from God. This makes sense as Moses was the one person that God spoke to personally (or face to face) when he wanted his words passed on to the people. In which case the rest of the Pentateuch may well have been compiled by others later from stories passed down orally and repeatedly retold until they were eventually collected together and committed to writing in the form we now have. This then both provides a framework for the Law of Moses which it contains, and also acts as a commentary upon it.

All this background detail may have seemed rather technical at times and hopefully not too overwhelming, but getting some idea of what was possibly read in the time of Nehemiah does help us gain a fuller understanding of what we have already seen so far in the book of Nehemiah. It will also help us in the rest of the chapters in this section.

Some final points before we end this chapter. What happened to this book of the Law which Moses wrote? Where was it kept? And what was its main intention? Why was a written copy necessary?

The first part of the answer is that it was passed on to Joshua, so that he could meditate on it day and night (Josh. 1:8). Moses was about to die and a new leader take over. Succession was important and when Moses was no longer around it would be vital to have a written record of what God had said to him. Joshua was now the one responsible for reminding the people what God required of them, so this Book of the Law was not to 'depart from his mouth', meaning that he had to keep speaking out these words and laws.

It is interesting also that Joshua added to it before he died, recording in it the covenant he made with the people at Shechem, including all the laws and decrees he drew up at that time (Josh. 24:25-26). It seems Joshua was a faithful keeper of the book and wanted to ensure that the heritage continued.

The second point is that the book itself was to be kept in a safe place. We learn in Deuteronomy 31:26 that this was to be next to the ark of the covenant, not *in* it but *beside* it. Of the Law, only the two tablets containing the Ten Commandments were to be placed inside the ark but the book had a special resting place next to it. However, what is particularly interesting in this verse is that the Book of the Law was to remain there as a witness or testimony *against* the people of Israel. This was its real purpose, to testify against them, and we will need to explore this more in further chapters in this section if we are to fully grasp the intention of the Law both then and now.

Meanwhile, in our next chapter we will focus on the one word we have been using all the time but without explaining its true meaning, namely Law or Torah.

Chapter Twenty-One

Torah

So far we have seen that the Book of the Law of Moses mentioned in Nehemiah may not have been exactly the same as any of the books in our Bible today. Rather it was most likely a separate book or scroll that Moses wrote in order to preserve all the words which God spoke to him personally and directly and which he (Moses) was to pass on to the people of God. This would include all the laws and decrees that God wanted Israel to know about and which we still have today contained within the first five books of our Bible, known as the Pentateuch.

We also saw that this Book of the Law (also called the Book of the Covenant) was to be placed next to the ark of the covenant and kept there as a testimony or witness *against* the Israelites, something which we will mention again later. In addition, after the death of Moses the responsibility for ensuring that its contents were frequently read to the Israelites was passed on to Joshua and it is a fair assumption that it continued to be handed down until the time of Ezra and Nehemiah.

In this chapter we want to explain the true meaning of the word 'Law' or 'Torah' and consider its role within the community of Israel.

What does the word 'Law' suggest to you? How do you feel when you hear the word? Usually what comes to mind is a legal system such as we have in this country, with its police force (the long arm of the Law!), courts, barristers, magistrates and judges. Here is a formidable array of those 'out to get us' the moment we step out of line. We know instinctively that something like this is necessary but it can also feel somewhat threatening and to be avoided.

This unfavourable image can spill over into our Bible reading. When we come across the word 'Law' we can have a negative reaction. We are glad that we are often told we are now free from the Law or not 'under' it, but without really knowing what this means. Clichéd phrases can often hide the real truth.

This negativity, or aversion to the Law, also creates a bit of a biblical dilemma, as we read in the scriptures that the Law is a delight (Ps. 1:2), and that among other things it revives the soul, makes wise the simple, gives joy to the heart and light to the eyes (Ps. 19:7-8). We are also aware that another Psalm (a very long one) is devoted entirely to extolling the virtues of the Law (Ps. 119).

We might decide this is fine within the Old Testament but no longer for us and we can leave it behind. But then we come across Paul in the New Testament describing the Law as holy, righteous, good and spiritual (Rom. 7:12, 14, 16). So the dilemma continues, and that's without considering some of the positive things Jesus said about the Law, which we will pick up in a later chapter.

The solution to all this is a proper understanding of the Hebrew word 'Torah' which is usually translated as

'Law'. But this is misleading. The word 'Torah' is better understood as guidance, direction, instruction, or simply teaching. It is about setting someone on the right path, or pointing someone in the right direction, showing them the way ahead.

Hebrew words are based upon a root system and those with identical or similar consonants have related meanings. This helps us understand a word much better. Torah is related to a word for guiding an arrow towards a target, making sure it hits the mark. From there other related words are derived, for instance those for an archer who shoots or directs the arrow, for a teacher who instructs a student and for a parent who guides or teaches a child until he or she is mature enough to make their own decisions wisely.

Now we have arrived at the heart of the matter. Torah (or Law) is best thought of in terms of a parent bringing up a child, someone who offers instruction and guidance into what is right and wrong, and explains the consequences of each choice. Rules and regulations are a necessary part of this. When raising children, we all use 'dos' and 'don'ts', and even the occasional 'and if you do, then...' But we also know that parenting is more than just issuing instructions and prohibitions. These come within a bigger package of loving care dedicated to helping youngsters grow up into responsible adults.

Once we realise this is the true meaning of the word 'Law' and its real purpose, we can see why in Hebraic thinking this is regarded as something positive. The Law is good. It's a joy, even wonderful, something to be welcomed rather than shunned or feared.

Torah comes from a loving heavenly parent and teacher who has our best interests at heart. God is not primarily a lawgiver but a caring Father who instructs and guides his children into the right way. He wants us to hit the target, not miss the mark. Does that phrase remind us of something?

In Romans 3:23 Paul says we have all sinned and fallen short, using a very Jewish idiom for describing sin. This idea of sin as 'falling short' or 'missing the mark' is a term from archery as an arrow fails to reach its target. Hebrew thinking often uses everyday ideas to express spiritual concepts, in this case sinfulness. Here, an arrow is speeding towards its goal, yet it fails to get there. It has deviated from its target or dropped to the ground well short. This is in contrast to Torah as teaching which guides us accurately and dependably towards the mark.

When we translate Torah as Law, or think of it in purely legalistic terms, we are 'falling short' in our understanding of what God is doing. If we interpret the Law as simply laws then we are restricting ourselves to only one part of its meaning. Even within the first five books of the Old Testament, which are collectively known as Torah, there is far more than just rules and regulations. There is a lot of narrative which is just as useful in providing guidance, and many stories which show us the right way to live and what happens when we choose otherwise. That is why to the Jewish mind the whole of their scripture, every book in our Old Testament, can be regarded as Torah or teaching.

It is also worth noting that even the Ten Commandments are not actually called commandments in the Hebrew text. They are just called 'words' (*devarim*). This is clear in Exodus

20:1, which precedes the so-called Ten Commandments, where it says, 'And God spoke all these words.' But it is equally the case in Deuteronomy 5:22, where you might find it translated as, 'These are the commandments' but where once again the Hebrew simply says, 'These are the words the Lord proclaimed.'

If you recall from the previous chapter, the book of Deuteronomy is actually entitled 'These are the words', rather than 'Here is my rule book'. It's as if God is really saying, 'Can I have word with you?' which under certain circumstances may still sound ominous, depending what you've just done!

So, in summary so far, if every time you see the word 'Law' in the Bible you think in terms of bringing up a child then you won't go far wrong. With this understanding of Torah, all the scriptures that mention 'Law' will make more sense and take on a deeper meaning.

There are still questions to consider regarding the Law in the New Testament scriptures and ourselves as New Covenant believers. We will save these to the next chapter. For now, we will turn our attention to the role of the Law with regard to ancient Israel and tie this in with our studies in Nehemiah.

We must start by correcting a common misunderstanding which is often assumed and repeatedly stated as fact, namely that the Law provided a means by which the Jewish people were saved, that it somehow brought them into a relationship with God that in our terms we call salvation. Let's be clear: it was never intended by God as such *and they knew it*.

Israel was in no doubt they were chosen out of God's inexplicable grace, mercy and love, and that faith (that is, trusting in what God said he would do for them) was the only way to relate to him, please him, or be counted as righteous. They had many examples of this from their past, such as Noah and Abraham. And above all, as we shall see in a moment, they had the experience of Passover and the Exodus.

Of course, once you are given rules there is always the temptation to think this is the way to be accepted. Don't we also think like this at times, that keeping the rules earns us merit or even gets us to heaven? That is certainly how people without faith might think. And being human, individual Jews no doubt fell into this trap also at times. However, to suggest that God provided the Law as a means of salvation for Israel is a big mistake. But this is often assumed either out of ignorance or a sense of Christian superiority – that was the old (Jewish) way, they were under the Law, now we know better. This view creates a false dichotomy or division within the whole Bible story, and deflects Christianity away from its true origins. It also reflects badly on God, suggesting he must have got it wrong and had to start again, as well as undermining the true nature of his fatherhood.

Israel knew that their liberation came before the Law. God had redeemed them first when he brought them out of slavery. They hadn't earned this or merited it in any way. All they had done was cry out to God (see Exod. 3:7-10).

Moreover, God rescued or 'saved' them, under the covenant he had previously made with Abraham, not under any new set of laws. God had even told Abraham in advance that his descendants would be enslaved in a foreign country for 400 years but that he would then release them (Gen. 15:13-14). So when Moses was called to lead God's people out of Egypt he knew this was because of God's previous dealings with Abraham. When God appeared to Moses in the burning bush he announced himself as the God of Abraham, Isaac and Jacob (Exod. 3:6). This was the God that Moses knew and the covenant he understood, one based upon faith and trust, not any laws.

The Israelites would be set free if they trusted in the Passover sacrifice they were told to make and were obedient concerning the application of blood to their doorposts. The Law would come later, after they had been redeemed by the blood of the lambs they had sacrificed and once they had been finally delivered from the Egyptians by the mighty hand of God acting on their behalf as they passed through the waters of the Red Sea.

The New Testament also teaches this perspective. Paul explains in Galatians chapter 3, a great passage on the Law to which we will return in our next chapter, that the Law was introduced or added 430 years after the promises made to Abraham. In covenant terms, which is a good way of understanding the whole biblical story, the Sinai or Mosaic covenant came long after the Abrahamic covenant but did not supersede or replace it. Rather it was added to it. The covenant with Abraham remained in place. Nor did the Law oppose God's earlier promises to Abraham. Rather the Law supplemented these but without changing the basis of righteousness which was still faith in what God had said (see Gal. 3:16-21).

So if the role of the Law was not to bring salvation or deliverance, what was it? There are two main purposes that stand out, based upon what we have already said about the true sense of the word Torah as teaching or direction and how it relates to the upbringing of a child.

For Israel, Sinai was the start of a new life with the God who had saved them. They had just been 'reborn' by the will of the father who loved them. Now they needed guidance or direction in how to grow up and live according to his ways. If they were to be part of his household, then these were the rules. Another similar way of looking at this is to see the Sinai covenant in terms of a marriage and vows taken. This is how the relationship was to work. If Israel wanted God's protection and provision then this is how they had to live as part of his family. In both these illustrations, the aim is the same. To show gratitude for what God had done for them, and to show off to the world what their father, or husband, was like.

But the other crucial role of the Law was to point to something beyond itself. This is vital to realise. Above all it means that the Law was given not to be *kept*, but to be *broken*. That sounds strange until you realise that its ultimate purpose was to lead Israel towards their Messiah, a necessary future saviour.

Repeatedly throughout the Pentateuch and beyond, every time laws were given they were broken. From the very beginning Adam breaks the one law he is given, and this merely involved *not* doing something. Indeed, at the same time as giving him this commandment, God told him he *would* break it – *when* you eat, he said, not *if* (Gen. 2:17). The tone had been set, the pattern would continue. From now on any law will be broken; not might be, but definitely will be.

By the end of his life Moses, having repeatedly called Israel to obedience, had no expectation that they ever would keep the Law. Indeed he prophesies further disobedience, curses and exile (see Deut. 31:14-30). And we have already seen that Nehemiah ends in similar disappointment and failure. The Law was repeatedly read but the people still went their own way rather than God's. This should not be a surprise. Given everything that had happened previously within the Old Testament story, it was inevitable.

In addition, recall that we said earlier that the Book of the Law of Moses was to be placed next to the ark of the covenant as a witness or testimony *against* Israel. Now we see why. It was a permanent reminder of Israel's inability to live up to its standards. This book could not ultimately make a real difference however many times it was read.

So was there another way out of this problem? Maybe the Law was trying to tell them something else?

Immediately after Adam's disobedience comes a promise that one day God will provide a solution (Gen. 3:15). Someone will come and put this right. The answer is not a book or another set of rules and regulations but a person, an offspring of Eve. Here was the one towards whom all this was heading, without whom it would all keep going wrong.

And so at the end of Nehemiah, and hence at the end of the Old Testament story, they were left waiting, waiting for Genesis 3:15 to come true, a wait that would last for another 400 years before their redemption would come.

We will pick this up in our next chapter, when we will look at what the New Testament says about the Law and consider what this means for us as New Covenant believers.

Chapter Twenty-Two

The Law of Moses and the New Testament

So far we have seen that the true meaning of Law, and therefore the correct translation of Torah, is that of guidance and direction. It relates to the upbringing of a child who needs certain rules to guide him into maturity and to teach him how to live within the family into which he has been born. Torah comes from a loving father not an angry lawmaker or judge.

We also saw that what we call the Law of Moses (as found within the first five books of our Bible) is not a system of salvation or righteousness and was never intended as such. It was given to Israel after their liberation in order to show them the will of their redeemer and to enable them to display him to the world, especially to those yet to experience what God could do for them.

With all this in mind we can now approach what the New Testament says about the Law, and start to gain an understanding of how this applies to believers within the New Covenant provided by Jesus. In the light of this covenant, certain issues inevitably arise but, with what we have seen so far, we have the necessary background to bring these into sharper focus and provide some observations and explanations. In particular we can tackle what for New Testament believers is perhaps the main question: is there any value for us in reading this Book of the Law of Moses today as they did in the time of Nehemiah? That is the aim of this chapter and the next, the final one in this section.

Questions regarding the Christian believer's relationship to the Law of Moses are common and plentiful. Basically, these questions revolve around whether the Law is still in effect or not, and if so, to what extent. It seems too much to say that it is still wholly in operation but somehow not quite right to assert that it has been completely discarded. Surely we are not to be lawless? Some of it, at least, still seems to apply. After all, isn't it the same Father God who must equally want to direct and guide those of us who since the advent of Christ have also been 'born again' into his family?

We have seen that at the end of Nehemiah there would be a 400-year gap before the next piece of God's revelation. In particular, Israel was left waiting for the promise of Genesis 3:15 to be fulfilled, namely that an offspring of Eve would come and deal with the consequences of Adam and Eve's disobedience. Once this happened, certain changes would inevitably follow, some of which would create a significant contrast with what had gone before. But in other areas there would not be such a dramatic change. Rather there would be more a sense of continuity or constancy, even if within this there were some smaller elements of change or development.

Understanding these twin concepts of contrast and continuity, and how they apply, is crucial when piecing together the various parts of the biblical story, especially in connecting its two main parts, the Old and New Testaments. Some might argue for a complete disconnection, a total reset. For others, this would destroy God's overall purpose and undermine his character. It might also make us worry where this would leave us if he decided on another new start.

In this matter of contrast and continuity, some topics are easier to sort out than others. For instance, the cross ended any further need for animal sacrifices. That was a huge change. But the nature and character of God must be a constant. This has to remain the same throughout scripture. A topic such as the Law, however, is much more complex and a simplistic answer won't do. It is too easy to fall into one of two errors: either everything has changed or nothing has changed. As we unpack certain New Testament texts we will gain a greater appreciation of how the apostles came to terms with this complexity.

It is worth starting with John 1:17 which simply states: 'For the law was given through Moses; grace and truth came through Jesus Christ.' That's in the New International Version. But some other versions, for example the Authorised or King James Version, adds another word in the middle: 'For the law was given by Moses, *but* grace and truth came through Jesus Christ. This 'but' makes a significant difference to how we read this, and it is not in the original Greek. It is a translational addition, put there to suggest, or even create, a contrast and break any continuity.

Was there really no truth before Jesus? Was God not gracious in the past? We've seen that his dealings with Israel, especially concerning the Exodus, were full of his grace. At least in some versions, such as the Authorised or King James Version, the word 'but' is in italics to acknowledge that it is absent in the Greek (watch out in general for italicised words in some versions). However, by including the 'but' even in italics means the damage is already done. It has also detached the meaning of this verse from that of the previous one, John 1:16, which reads: 'From the fullness of his grace we have all received one blessing after another.'[2] Put these two verses together and the apostle is rejoicing over a succession of blessings which have flowed from God's gracious hand. First there was the Law given through Moses, what a blessing that was, and then we were blessed even more when Jesus came and brought more truth. Here is grace upon grace, one blessing after another. There was a difference over time as God's plan progressed, but please, 'but me no buts'!

Let's turn next to Paul, someone who knew more about the Law than most, and who came to know Christ better than most of us ever will. What did he have to say on this matter?

In his first letter to Timothy, Paul wrote, 'We know that the law is good if one *uses it properly*' (1 Tim. 1:8, italics mine). That's an interesting statement. How do we 'use it properly'? We saw in an earlier chapter that Paul still regarded the Law as good, as well as holy, righteous and spiritual (Rom. 7:12, 14, 16). But what is its true purpose?

Paul asks this very question in Galatians 3:19, 'What, then, was the purpose of the law?'[3] When Paul asks a question in a letter we can safely assume he is about to answer it

2. NIV 1984 version.
3. NIV 1984 version.

himself. He is not waiting for a reply by return of post, or saying 'answers on a postcard, please'! We commented in our previous chapter that in Galatians chapter 3 Paul explains how the Law was part of the Sinai covenant, which was added to the one God made 430 years previously with Abraham, and that the Law did not replace this covenant or oppose the promises made in it.

We now also see in this verse (Gal. 3:19), Paul explaining why it was added. It was necessary because of Adam's initial transgression which led to continual further transgressions among the whole of humanity, and because the solution, that promised Seed or offspring of Genesis 3:15, had not yet come. Moses, for all his calling and qualities, was not that fulfilment. And so, Paul concludes, in Galatians 3:24, that the purpose of the law was to be put in charge to lead us to Christ. It supervised us, or looked after us, until he came and we could put our faith in him. Older versions often translate this as the Law being like a schoolmaster or tutor, which fits perfectly with the idea of Torah being a guide or teacher, or anyone bringing up a child, which we looked at in a previous chapter.

Paul recognises that being under this 'schoolmaster' might feel somewhat harsh at times, even a bit like being a prisoner, locked up for a while (Gal. 3:23). But it was for our good, holding us fast until we could be passed on to a 'better' teacher. Paul could see where all this has been heading. Torah was indeed pointing beyond itself, and ultimately faith in Christ provides the kind of supervision and guidance we really need.

That is why in Romans 10:4 Paul can say that Christ is the end of the law so that there may be righteousness for everyone who believes. But this is also often misunderstood.

'End' is taken to mean finished, all over, so it is assumed that this verse is telling us that Christ has put an end to the law completely. But the Greek word for end, *telos*, signifies something quite different. Its real meaning refers to the goal, aim or objective of something.

'*Telos*' was a term already found in Aristotle's philosophical works where he talks of the 'actualisation of inherent purpose'. That's quite a phrase. Basically he is saying that *telos* signifies the ultimate purpose of something and how this is brought into reality. From this we get the modern term 'teleology' which is the study of an object together with its aims, purposes or intentions.

So Paul is saying in Romans 10:4 that the objective of the Law is to show us Christ, and that he is the goal of the Torah as a whole. Moreover, to call Christ the *telos* of the Torah (to mix together a bit of Greek and Hebrew!) indicates that we are not to expect anything further. There is no-one else to come afterwards in relation to this particular matter.

With Christ, the Law has reached its end point, or its full extension. But this does not mean it is now fit only to be thrown away or discarded completely. Its main job is over but it can still be useful in some way within the New Torah of Jesus. As an illustration, though perhaps not a perfect one, when a train reaches its destination (or terminus) it does not suddenly disappear. But its journey is over. It has delivered us to the right place. The driver can now get out and take a rest. Someone else can take over.

What else can Paul tell us about the Christian and the Law? Can he clarify what is meant when we say we are 'free' from the Law or not 'under' the Law?

Paul uses the phrase 'under the law' many times, especially in his letter to the Romans. But the best place to start is in Galatians 3:25 where we find the full phrase 'under the supervision of the law'.[4] As we have seen, Paul is saying there that for the Christian believer our supervisor has changed. So if in Paul's writings we come across the shorter version 'under the law' then in our minds at least we should add the idea of supervision and recognise this is going back to the original purpose of the Law until Christ came.

Another important passage is 1 Corinthians 9:19-23 which is full of phrases involving the words 'free' and 'under'. Try picking your way through all that! It can seem that Paul is contradicting himself at times. In 1 Corinthians 9:20, he says, 'though I myself am not under the law', while in verse 21 he states, 'though I am not free from God's law but am under Christ's law'. How confusing! But we can now understand that Paul is trying to explain what it is like when the essence of Torah stays the same but the tutor or supervisor changes. To pick up our earlier illustration, Paul is now on the Jesus train not the Moses train. Some of the carriages may look the same but it is being driven by a different person.

So what does 'free' mean in this context? In summary, what we as Christians need to be free from is the law as an impersonal system that makes demands upon us which we cannot keep and which therefore leads to condemnation. To this end, Paul talks about dying to the Law. It's that dramatic. But it is the only way to be free from its demands. Read Romans 7:1-6 for more on this, and note especially

---

4. NIV 1984 version.

verse 6, which says, 'By dying to what once bound us, we have been released from the law so that we serve in the new way of the Spirit and not in the old way of the written code.' Christian freedom is not ultimately about freedom from the Law but from sin and self, and there is a new Torah for this.

One reason why Paul's writing on the Law can seem complicated is that he is often struggling over the language involved. This is equally true of our English translations. Paul uses the word 'Law' in several different ways: to refer to the entire Hebrew scriptures, or more specifically to the Law given through Moses, or sometimes to reflect a legalistic interpretation of God's commands. In the Greek of his day there was no actual word for legalism so Paul had to use phrases like 'under the law' or 'works of the law', or sometimes simply 'law' itself to express this wrong attitude. This has led some to assume that the law itself is bad or totally wrong.

Then there is the additional complication of working out whether Paul is writing specifically to the Jews (who had the Mosaic Law) or to Gentiles (who didn't but who still had some understanding of what law meant) or to both.

Whole books have been written on Paul and the Law, so this has just been a sketch of the main ideas, but hopefully enough to help us understand the basic truths and to provide a framework for our New Testament reading.

In our final chapter in this section, we will turn to Jesus and some of the things he said. We will also see how Pentecost fits into all this, and consider some of the ways we can benefit from reading the Book of the Law of Moses today as they did in the time of Nehemiah.

Chapter Twenty-Three

Jesus, Pentecost and the Law of Moses

So far we have seen that Law or Torah relates to the upbringing of children or the guidance of students and that this is consistent throughout the Old and New Testaments. We have also looked at several passages in Paul's letters, but as yet have not considered anything that Jesus said. So let's start by putting this right.

One of the best-known remarks by Jesus on the Law is when he said he hadn't come to abolish it but to fulfil it (Matt. 5:17). But it is far less well known what he was actually saying. It is often assumed that by 'fulfil' he meant he was bringing it to a complete end, which we saw in the last chapter was not the case, and wouldn't anyway be consistent with what he said in the next verse, Matthew 5:18, about not one single bit of it disappearing. Another assumption is that 'fulfil' means he would keep every bit of it perfectly. We will come back to this in a moment, but again it is not what he is saying here.

Although to fulfil something can bring it to a finish (as in fulfilling a promise or a prophecy), in this context (the so-called Sermon on the Mount) Jesus is operating as a teacher explaining what and how he will teach. In particular he is a Jewish teacher talking to Jewish people who would readily understand his use of the words 'fulfil' and 'abolish'. Both terms are Jewish idioms. An idiom is a word or expression that has a specific, usually non-literal, meaning within its own language which doesn't translate directly into another. For instance, we might say it's raining cats and dogs without referring in any way to our pets.

Within the context of teaching, to 'abolish' the Law, or indeed any single law, is to undermine it through incorrect or inadequate interpretation. By not teaching its proper meaning it is essentially rendered ineffective. It is not being repealed or annulled, but if people don't know what it is really about then they cannot obey it and so to them it becomes 'abolished'.

By contrast, to 'fulfil' the Law, or any single law, means to teach the correct meaning or interpretation. Only then is it possible for someone to be obedient to it. In this sense the root meaning of fulfil is 'to cause to stand' or 'place on a correct footing'. This is what Jesus promised to do to the Law at the outset of his ministry and which we see he did straightaway in the rest of Matthew chapters 5 to 7. He will take the Law and fill it full of meaning, full to the brim in fact. Those listening to Jesus knew exactly what he was saying in Matthew 5:17. They were used to hearing the various laws debated, with one teacher accusing another, 'You are abolishing that law!' 'No! I'm fulfilling it,' might be the reply.

For Jesus, like Paul and all the apostles, the Law or Torah was good and holy. Jesus believed it revealed God's will and taught God's guidance for daily life. His high esteem for Torah meant he was dedicated to upholding it and interpreting it correctly. He was going to help us get at its true meaning.

We said earlier that some think 'fulfil' meant Jesus would keep the whole Law perfectly. But that's rather strange. To be pedantic, Jesus couldn't keep all the laws anyway as some applied only to women or to priests. But of more relevance is the fact that he didn't share our sinful nature in any way. His relationship with the Father was perfect at all times. So in that sense he didn't break any laws but it is difficult to say that he kept them either. So does the Law even apply to Jesus at all? If the purpose of the Law was to lead sinful men to Christ, how could it lead the sinless Christ to himself?! Perhaps we should say that Jesus was permanently 'above the Law'. This is just a tentative suggestion but it may be part of the reason why only he could interpret or teach the Law properly.

The other well-known remark of Jesus regarding the Law is his reply to the question, 'Which is the greatest commandment?' This was a common question to Jewish teachers of the time, and they had to have an answer. Jesus' twofold reply involves love: loving God and loving others (Matt. 22:36-40). But Jesus is not saying that love has replaced the Law or any of the laws. On the contrary. Jesus added that all the Law hangs on (or depends on) these two, so all these other laws must still be in place. We will return to this comment of Jesus later.

Let's now move on to Pentecost, also called the Feast of Weeks. This was one of the three main feasts that God told Israel to celebrate (Lev. 23:15-22). It is not usually known that this feast became associated with the giving of the Law at Sinai. It is difficult to date precisely when Moses received the Law but it was certainly around seven weeks or fifty days after the Exodus. But it must be noted that nowhere in scripture is Pentecost linked with the giving of the Law. This was a later rabbinic tradition so we cannot assume Jesus or the disciples associated the Day of Pentecost with the Mosaic Law, though the similarity in the dating and other parallels suggest this connection is not unreasonable.

Moreover, there is a pertinent link between the giving of the Holy Spirit and the Law of God. Jeremiah chapter 31 tells us about God's intention to make a new covenant with Israel. Part of this was to put his Law in their minds and write it on their hearts (Jer. 31:31-33). The Law was to be internalised rather than being on tablets of stone or merely in a book. This was to be the role of the Holy Spirit within a believer. So the reason why we should not steal, commit adultery, murder and so on, is not because these are written in a book of rules, or even in the New Testament scriptures, but because of the internal working of the Holy Spirit in our lives, which is why all believers should be filled with the Spirit.

As an illustration, consider the Highway Code. This is written in a book to be learnt, but it has to be internalised if you are to drive safely, both for yourself and others. There's no time when driving along to consult it every time you need to make a decision. Nor would this be particularly safe either.

Jesus promised to send us the Holy Spirit to lead us into all truth, part of which is to parent us or guide us into the new Law or Torah of Christ. Perhaps we should rediscover this element of Pentecost when we celebrate this day in our churches or Christian communities.

As we close this section let's draw together some of these strands and in particular come back to the main point of how we today should read the Book of the Law of Moses (or its equivalent within our Old Testament). Paul declared that all scripture is God-breathed (or inspirational) and useful for teaching, rebuking, correcting and training in righteousness (2 Tim. 3:16). This must include the Law of Moses so let's look at some ways in which it can be useful.

Fundamental to all this is to remember that the primary function of the Law is still to lead people to Christ, the one who can teach it properly. So it can, and should, be used to preach the gospel. After telling us that the Law is good if used properly, Paul explains it is made for lawbreakers and rebels, the ungodly and sinful, the unholy and irreligious (1 Tim. 1:9). The Law can be used by the Holy Spirit to convict people of sin and point them to their Saviour. Just as the book of the Law of Moses was placed next to the ark of the covenant as a testimony against Israel, so the Law continues to testify against people today. It acts as a prosecuting attorney, making us acutely aware of our need but also showing us that this is a problem that it was not ultimately designed to fix.

So the Law continues to function as inspired scripture that teaches, informs and instructs. But it now has a dual purpose. It operates in two slightly different but related ways. Its original purpose remains for unbelievers, to show their need for a Saviour, but for believers meditating on the Law reminds us of Christ and what he has done for us.

It should inspire gratitude as it reminds us of the power of sin and death, of all that we have been saved from.

Some would say that the Old Testament largely contains shadows and that the reality or substance is found in Christ and the New Testament. This is true in lots of ways as the writer to the Hebrews constantly explains. The tabernacle, for instance, was a copy of something heavenly, and, in its original form, would ultimately be replaced, though the purpose and meaning that it reflected would remain. As another example, the whole system of sacrifices, ceremonial washings and the Levitical priesthood were not designed to last forever. All were shadows pointing to something better to come.

But shadows can still be useful. They have the right shape. They outline the object itself and are connected to it. You are never totally detached from your own shadow. So even now that we have the realities, or substance, the shadows in the Law continue not only to point to the Messiah (for those who still need this) but also to help us who have accepted him to understand him better. The cross makes more sense in the light of previous sacrifices. The old Temple informs us about ourselves as the new Temple of God, and so on. This is how the New Testament writers saw all this, and how they taught on it.

That's all fine in general but we still have to come to terms with all those individual laws! Let's start by going back to what Jesus said about the greatest commandment being to love God and others, and how all the Law hangs on these (Matt. 22:36-40). If love is the beating heart of all the commandments, then every time we read one of them we should ask how this helps us love God more or love others better. Find the love aspect of each law. This might still be tricky at times but it's a good start. Remember, though, that in the Bible love is not primarily an emotion but a matter of the will, about making choices. To love God is to put him first. To love others is to put them above yourself. So ask, how does this law help me make the right choice? How does it counter my natural selfishness and lack of love?

After finding the love in each law, look for the theology. Torah as a whole is an expression of God's character, so ask, how does this law reflect the nature of an unchanging God? What does it say about his holiness? Or his jealousy? In that sense, the Law functions theologically, so meditating on it will help us know God better.

Then look for the wisdom in each law. The Law as a whole is an expression of God's great wisdom and is capable of making us wise. We can then show this wisdom to others around us. In one place, Moses said to the people, concerning God's laws, 'Observe them carefully, for this will show your wisdom and understanding to the nations, who will hear all about these decrees and say, "Surely this great nation is a wise and understanding people"' (Deut. 4:6).

In the New Testament Paul twice quotes Deuteronomy 25:4 about not muzzling an ox while it is treading out the grain. Paul argues that the wisdom in this law was not for the ox's sake only. 'Is it about oxen that God is concerned?' he queries. 'Surely he says this for us, doesn't he?' So Paul applies it to Christian workers also (1 Cor. 9:9; 1 Tim. 5:18). The argument is that if it meant that then, how much more does it mean for us now. Certainly, meditating on the Law should mean we live more wisely and make better decisions.

With any Old Testament law we should remember the original context is that of a new nation recently set free from centuries of slavery and now being asked to live for God amid pagan people. They needed appropriate laws for that purpose, specific to them then. Some of these aren't necessarily for all people for all times, at least not in the form then given. God met Israel where they were and gave them some baby steps to follow. Like any good parent, he taught them to walk before running. This is early learning, initial lessons in holiness and right living. Some have even compared this to a kindergarten.

Also worth remembering is that all the laws were not given at the same time. As the story of Israel developed, laws were added, such as the wearing of tassels (Num. 15:37-41). The more they sinned, the more laws they needed to guide them, just as a father might impose extra rules on a wayward teenager.

One final point which might help. Think of Israel as the first child in a family, and us as the second. Do parents bring up the second child in the same way? Largely yes, because it is the same family. But there might also be slight differences for a variety of reasons.

To sum up, the Law or Torah is not obsolete or redundant even for those who trust Jesus as their Saviour. It still helps those who belong to Christ to know the right way to live, even though it cannot produce righteousness. The Law has to work alongside faith, without stepping in its place, or taking over. If it does either of these then the fault is ours not that of the Law or its giver.

There are two extremes to warn against. One is to oppose Torah in the belief that this might put some people 'under the law'. The other is to become over-zealous in law keeping and fall into a religiosity that lacks the intimate leading of the Holy Spirit. Both of these are incorrect and harmful in their own way. But if we can avoid these then we can continue to read what God gave to Moses with purpose and benefit.

Section 3

The Feast of Tabernacles

Chapter Twenty-Four

Moedim

In Part One, we learnt from Nehemiah chapter 8 that one of the results of the Israelites reading the Book of the Law of Moses was the rediscovery of the Feast of Tabernacles. In particular that they were to live in booths (or tabernacles) for a seven-day period during the seventh month. In their desire to be obedient to all that they were reading, they immediately set about putting this into practice, especially as this feast was due in a few days' time. The result was great joy (see Neh. 8:13-17).

But what exactly were they celebrating and how? And does this mean anything for us today or can we just leave it in the pages of scripture as something no longer relevant? In the next few chapters we shall see that this feast was immensely significant at the time of Jesus and that he related to it in several revealing and powerful ways. Once we realise this then our understanding of Jesus is greatly enhanced with perhaps some surprises along the way. We will also uncover something about our future once Jesus has returned to Earth, so perhaps we too ought to rediscover the Feast of Tabernacles.

I say 'rediscover' not 'discover' as this feast, like all our Jewish roots, was once part of the community of Christian believers. But early on in church history this heritage began to be dismissed and even dismantled to avoid any connection with the Jewish people who were then seen as being 'a cursed nation'. For example, the Council of Caesarea at the end of the second century AD changed the celebration of Jesus' resurrection from the third day of Passover (called Firstfruits) to the feast of the pagan fertility goddess Ishtar or Eostre. By the fourth century, the Council of Nicaea under Constantine made all such changes official and outlawed any previous observances. Persecution followed to stamp them out completely and Christianity became greatly impoverished by being detached from its roots and transplanted into foreign soil.

The Israelites in Nehemiah's day had equally lost something by not celebrating the Feast of Tabernacles, but this was due to it being forgotten not outlawed, temporarily mislaid rather than discarded. What then might they have read in the Book of the Law of Moses that made them realise what they were missing?

As we said in a previous chapter, we can't be precisely sure what this Book of the Law was like but we can reasonably assume that, if they read about the Feast of Tabernacles, it contained at least one of the following: Leviticus 23:33-43, Deuteronomy 16:13-15, or the more detailed Numbers 29:12-39. These are key passages so it would be worth pausing to read them now or make a note to follow them up later.

In addition there is a reference in Exodus 23:16, where it is called the Feast of Ingathering as it occurred in the seventh month (or Tishrei), the time of the gathering or harvesting of crops. But this occasion was to be more than just a harvest festival. Its aim was to remind the Israelites of the time when they had wandered in the desert for forty years just after coming out of Egypt. All through this period God had looked after them though all they had to live in were temporary shelters, tent-like structures known as booths or tabernacles. It is this which gives the Feast its other name of Sukkot (Succoth), the plural of *sukkah* which means 'booth' or 'shelter'.

In the above passages, the Israelites were instructed to celebrate a festival to the Lord for seven days with an extra eighth day added on at the end (see Num. 29:12, 35; Lev. 23:36). In this period they were to re-enact the time their ancestors spent in the wilderness by making booths of their own and living in them for the week. This is typically how the Jewish people remembered their past. They recreated it by taking part in something similar, the aim being to experience it anew for themselves and keep it alive for future generations.

So this is what the Israelites in Nehemiah's day would have read about and realised they should do. We will look at more details from these passages later and see then what exactly occurred in this time, but for now let's put the Feast of Tabernacles in its wider context of the Jewish calendar and the feasts as a whole, as all these would feature significantly not only during the lifetime of Jesus but also within his own life.

There are three main annual feasts which eventually became known as the Pilgrim Feasts as this was when people made special journeys to Jerusalem to celebrate them and worship the Lord there. These are Passover (or Pesach), Pentecost (or Shavuot, also known as Weeks) and

Tabernacles (or Succoth). But overall there are seven feasts in the full cycle, perhaps because seven often represents perfection and completion. These seven occur in two clusters. The first three come in the first month (Nisan) with the fourth in the third month (Sivan). The last three take place in the seventh month (Tishrei). So they are not spread evenly over the year but occur during the two drier periods of the year, which may have been helpful for those making the pilgrimages in later times.

For the record here is the full list with their dates.

Passover (or Pesach) on the fourteenth of Nisan is followed by the Feast of Unleavened Bread from the fifteenth to the twenty-first of Nisan. This includes Firstfruits on the sixteenth of Nisan.

Then comes Pentecost (Shavuot or Weeks) on the sixth of Sivan, the third month, which completes the first cluster.

Then in the seventh month there is the Feast of Trumpets on the first of Tishrei, the Day of Atonement (Yom Kippur) on the tenth of Tishrei, and Tabernacles (or Succoth) from the fifteenth to the twenty-first of Tishrei. We shall see later how Tabernacles relates to the other two in the same cluster.

Perhaps the reason we are more familiar with the first cluster, known as the Spring Feasts, is because we can see they have meaning, even fulfilment, in the life of Jesus. We shall see later that the Autumn Feasts also take on a greater meaning, and fulfilment, when they too are considered in that same context.

We have been repeatedly calling these events 'feasts', which is correct in one way but does not convey the full meaning. In Leviticus chapter 23 they are repeatedly referred to as 'appointed' feasts or 'appointed times'. In Hebrew, this is *moedim*. This expression can be found in Leviticus 23:2 and 23:4, and then again towards the end in verses 37 and 44. You can't miss it! But notice that these are the appointed feasts *of the Lord*. They are his feasts, not Jewish feasts as such. They are God's appointed times which he gave first to the Jewish people but also to us, in the same way that the Torah was first given to Israel but also remains for us under the new covenant though with a greater meaning and significance. See the previous section on the Book of the Law of Moses for more on this.

So these feasts are not to be seen merely as part of Judaism and so to be left there without further consideration. They belong primarily to God. He calls them 'my appointed feasts' (Lev. 23:2). This should change the way we think about them, as appointments on his calendar and for his purposes.

The Hebrew word used, *moedim*, is the plural of *mo'ed* which occurs over 200 times in the Old Testament to refer to something that is appointed or fixed, usually in time but equally it can apply to a place of appointment such as the Tent of Meeting or Tabernacle in the wilderness.

Mo'ed derives from the root *ya'ad* meaning 'to fix by agreement' and hence by implication to meet at a stated time. It can be used, for instance, to summon someone to court for a trial, or to direct them to a certain place at a certain time for an important event such as a wedding. *Moedim* are times not to be missed, at least not without missing out on something important!

The first use of this word is in Genesis 1:14 where we are told that the sun and moon were created to mark or designate the seasons. These lights in the sky regulate our calendar so that we live in days, months and years. These seasons are now fixed for us as part of God's continual intervention on earth among men. We could ignore them but we cannot change them. Our only real choice is to align ourselves with them if we are to benefit from living in his creation.

The same goes for the *moedim* that make up the appointed feasts. They remain in place however much mankind may choose to create other festivals to replace them or devise new calendars to suit their own purposes. Moreover, the biblical calendar as expressed through the *moedim* helps us to recognise how worldly systems and pagan influences have infiltrated Christianity over the centuries. Separation from these becomes more possible once we realise there are alternatives which come from God himself.

As a slight aside, but one that is very instructive, consider Jeroboam's rebellion recorded in 1 Kings chapter 12. When the kingdom of Israel split after the death of King Solomon, his son Rehoboam was the rightful successor to the throne. But Jeroboam wanted to establish an alternative, separate from the house of David. To that end, he made two golden calves and set them up in Bethel and Dan as places of worship in competition with the Temple in Jerusalem. He also appointed non-Levitical priests and then instituted a festival on the fifteenth day of the eighth month, *a month of his own choosing* (1 Kgs 12:33). This was not one of God's appointed times, but something new which came out of dissension, disobedience and rebellion. We cannot actually replace what God has established, but often we put unhelpful or ungodly substitutes in their place. We must be very careful not to go against God's 'appointments' and think that by creating something new we have somehow made spiritual progress.

It is important to add that God's *moedim* are far more than just dates on a timetable. They are also described as 'sacred assemblies' or sometimes as 'holy convocations' (Lev. 23:2, 3, 37). The Hebrew word here is *mikrah*, which can also be thought of as a rehearsal. These festivals are like dress rehearsals, acted out in readiness for the main performance, which will occur when the Messiah makes an appearance on the earth's stage. As such there is a rich prophetic symbolism in God's *moedim* which contain great significance historically and spiritually. They outline God's redemptive plan as well as acting as reminders of what he has done and what he is still going to do.

By giving his people these appointed times God showed his desire to meet with them in specific ways in order to deepen their walk with him and keep them close to him. We can benefit from them in the same way. By engaging with the *moedim*, faith is built up and our understanding of Jesus is greatly enriched. This is what rediscovering our origins and reconnecting with our Jewish heritage is all about. For instance, in John's Gospel it has been calculated that about 75 per cent of the verses are directly related to events that occurred at the feasts. This shows how difficult it is to read the Gospels correctly without a knowledge of the *moedim*. We shall pick this up in a later chapter when we see what happened when Jesus attended the Feast of Tabernacles. Meanwhile, in our next chapter we will concentrate on what we are told about this feast from the Old Testament and how it applied to the Israelites.

Chapter Twenty-Five

Israel

In the previous chapter we put the Feast of Tabernacles within the larger context of the biblical calendar and saw that it was one of God's 'appointed times' or *moedim*. We will now look at its main features and consider how Israel has observed it in practice, all this in preparation for our remaining chapters when we will see how Jesus brought a deeper meaning to this feast and why we should not disregard it today.

We said earlier that Tabernacles was the third and final feast of the cluster of Autumn Feasts which occur in Tishrei, the seventh month. To appreciate one feature of this feast we should work our way through the month towards it. The first day of Tishrei is Rosh Hashanah (New Year) and is heralded by the sound of trumpets, hence its alternative name of Yom HaTruah (Day or Feast of Trumpets). This is a call to reflection and self-examination, and initiates the so-called Ten Days of Awe which culminates in the Day of Atonement (Yom Kippur). This period, from the first to the tenth of Tishrei, is a time of deep repentance and prayer, with Yom Kippur being the most solemn day of all. This is not just a period of confession but of actively correcting wrongs. It is seen as a time of dying but also of rebirth. By the end, the gates of forgiveness have been opened and the restoration of *shalom* or oneness has occurred. This should lead to thanksgiving and great rejoicing, and it does!

After a short gap of four days comes Tabernacles (or Succoth), from the fifteenth to the twenty-first of Tishrei. Several biblical texts command joy at this time (Lev. 23:40, Deut. 16:14-15). After the previous solemnity with all its introspection and repentance, this is now to be a time of unrestrained joy, such as if a victory has been won over an enemy in battle. It is no wonder that the rabbis have called Tabernacles 'the season of our joy'.

This is a celebration of forgiveness, one which recognises that true rejoicing is only possible after true repentance. But once you are assured that God has forgiven you, then you can be filled with a joy that surpasses all others. This joy is so overwhelming that it lasts for seven whole days, and even that is not enough so an extra eighth day is added. The seventh day is called the Great Hosanna (Hoshana Rabbah), which is a fitting climax to the week. But then comes the extra day, Simchat Torah, which means 'rejoicing over the Law'.

It has been said that 'he who has not seen Jerusalem during the Feast of Tabernacles does not know what rejoicing means'. A slight exaggeration perhaps but it makes the point. We can also now see why in Nehemiah 8:17 when they rediscovered Tabernacles 'their joy was very great'.

Tabernacles is also called the Feast of Thanksgiving as it coincides with the final harvest of the year. The success of another year's farming resulted in gratitude to God as well as being another reason to rejoice.

There are three main features of the Feast of Tabernacles for us to consider. One is the building of the booths. The others are water and light, in particular the water libation or offering and the brilliant illumination of the Temple.

As we said earlier, the purpose behind the Israelites building booths and living in them for seven days was to remember, and in some small way re-enact, the time their ancestors lived in temporary shelters while wandering in the wilderness just after the Exodus. So if the booth, or *sukkah*, was to provide a similar experience it had to be built according to certain rules or procedures.

Sukkah means 'woven' which gives a clue as to its construction. It had to be built outdoors and made from parts of trees or plants still in their natural state, so for instance boards or planks of wood could not be used. Moreover, these natural materials could not still be growing. So a whole tree, bush or hedge still in the place where it was planted was not allowed. Anything that was to be used had to be detached, cut off or uprooted.

The *sukkah* was to consist of only three sides, with the fourth side left open. The roof was also to be made of natural items like branches and leaves but not so densely woven that rain could not get through in places. Basically the *sukkah* had to be open in some way to the night sky, the test being that on a cloudless night some of the stars would be visible.

A *sukkah* was made in this way from natural elements to reflect God as creator, and its somewhat flimsy and fragile nature was to remind those living there that trusting in God was preferable to the solidity and comfort of their normal dwelling.

Succoth is still celebrated by many today in Israel and around the world. Families often start building their *sukkah* as soon as Yom Kippur is over. Some will live in it for the whole period of the feast, though others might just sleep there or take their meals in it. A token effort rather than the full commitment!

Another important element of the Feast of Tabernacles was light. In the Court of the Women within the Temple area, four large oil lamps or *menorah* were erected for the occasion. They were lit at the beginning of the feast and kept going for all eight days. At fourteen-feet high, ladders were needed to enable the oil to be replenished and the wicks trimmed. But being at this great height meant that the whole area was illuminated, with the light being seen all around Jerusalem and even to the hills beyond.

There were also daily torch-lit processions leading onto the Temple mount. These increased in size each day until on the last day, the Great Hosanna, there were so many people bearing torches that the light carried for miles around. We shall see in the next chapter how the theme of light was picked up by Jesus when he attended the Feast of Tabernacles.

Of equal interest to us is the significance of water as part of this feast. Each day saw a ceremony called the water libation or offering. A specially appointed Levitical priest (or some say the high priest himself) went to the Pool of Siloam with a golden pitcher and filled it with water, about two pints in total. He then returned to the Temple and poured the water into a basin at the foot of the altar as a special offering. This ritual of water pouring lasted throughout the whole of the seven-day feast and came to a climax on the seventh day, the Day of the Great Hosanna. On this final day the priest was accompanied on his journey to and from the Pool of Siloam by a large procession of people playing various musical instruments, enhanced by trumpet blasts and singing by the Levites, most probably Psalms 113-118.

Overall, this was a time of high drama and great excitement, hence another famous, though again one could argue rather overhyped, rabbinic statement that 'he who has not witnessed the joy of the water drawing has never in his life experienced real joy'. What's so exciting about pouring out water? Perhaps it was one of those things you just had to be there to understand. But it did have several possible meanings.

Some said it represented the knowledge of God covering the earth as the waters cover the sea. Others suggested that it acted as a reminder of their time in the desert and the lack of water until Moses struck the rock with Aaron's rod, another example of God's provision without which they wouldn't have survived. But more likely it was done in gratitude for the rain that had produced the recent harvest together with a prayer for more rain to come as summer was now at an end and the rainy season was needed again.

But there was also a prophetic and more spiritual aspect to the water ceremony. It became part of the messianic hope attached to this feast, in particular an expectation of the outpouring of the Spirit of God, and not just on Israel but on the whole world. This is something else to bear in mind when we come to our next chapter.

There are two further items we must mention: the *etrog* (or *ethrog*) and the *lulav*. Strange words! But easily understandable. In Leviticus 23:40 we read that the Israelites were to take choice fruit from the trees, as well as palm fronds, leafy branches and poplars, and rejoice (there's that word again) before the Lord. It was eventually decided that this choice fruit was to be the *etrog* or citron, a large yellow lemon-like fruit but one which was more fragrant and tastier than the usual lemon. Every Jew would bring one with them to the Temple as something symbolic of the fruit of the Promised Land.

As for the *lulav*, this was made up of bits of palm branches, myrtle and willow, all tied together with a golden thread to form a tightly bound cluster. This was also taken to the Temple to be waved before the Lord as an act of thanksgiving. Holding both your *etrog* and your *lulav*, you would dance round the altar waving the *lulav* in all four directions (north, east, south and west) as well as up and down, all to signify that the Lord your God is the God of everywhere. In contrast to regional deities who were associated only with local harvests, Yahweh is the God of the whole earth and of all harvests everywhere.

As for the scriptures, the book designated to be read at this feast was Ecclesiastes. This seems a strange choice for such a joyful occasion, but it was seen as sensible to balance out the joy with a reminder that life isn't always like this. In addition to Ecclesiastes the usual cycle of Torah readings (that's from the first five books) continued, and was both brought to a conclusion and started up again on the same day. So on the eighth day of the feast, known as Simchat Torah or the rejoicing over the Law, Deuteronomy chapters 33 and 34 were read and then followed with Genesis 1:1 – 2:3. This was to show that reading the Torah was a continual cycle which should never come to an end. It was a great honour to be the one called to read these portions in the synagogue on that day.

Simchat Torah was almost an extra celebration in its own right. This day, together with the first day of the feast, were always regarded as special Sabbaths, whichever day of the week they fell on. In synagogues today the Torah scrolls are lifted high as part of a procession as people dance around them singing joyful songs. Here is another explosion of joy as the synagogue becomes a place of great exuberance.

As for the sacrifices made at the Feast of Tabernacles, there were many. Numbers 29:13 onwards explains how many bulls, rams, lambs and goats were to be sacrificed. For instance, there were to be 13 bulls sacrificed on the first day, 12 on the second, and so on, until 7 on the seventh day. This is a total of 70, a number which in the Jewish mind symbolises the number of Gentile nations. The rabbis explain that this sacrifice of 70 bulls was actually being made on behalf of the other nations of the world, looking forward towards their conversion and gathering to God. This feast is the only one with a Gentile dimension, something the Jews felt they could share with the rest of the world. In addition to the 70 bulls, they sacrificed 14 rams and 98 lambs. This is five times as many bulls as for Passover, and double the number of rams and lambs.

We have only been able to give a brief account of what this feast came to signify over time. You can explore this in more detail for yourself. Much has been written elsewhere, in books and online.

Some of these aspects developed over the centuries, but by the time of Jesus all this was in place, seemingly waiting for him. In particular the whole occasion had gained a special messianic expectation. Perhaps this was the time when the Messiah would make an appearance?

We said this was a pilgrim festival. By the time of Jesus hundreds of thousands of people came up to Jerusalem for this feast. Many camped around the city on places such as the Mount of Olives. Jerusalem was more crowded than at any other time of the year. Let's now join this crowd and go to the Feast of Tabernacles with Jesus, for what would be the last time in his life.

Chapter Twenty-Six

Jesus

So far we have looked at how the Feast of Tabernacles fits into the whole calendar as one of God's appointed times or *moedim*, and then examined the many different features of it. We saw that joy dominates the feast: the joy of being forgiven after repentance, joy over the Law and the joy of a successful harvest. In addition, we mentioned the important role that water and light play in the celebrations, as well as the many sacrifices made with the Gentile nations in mind. We ended with the comment that this had become the time of year when messianic expectation was at its height. Might this be the year when the Messiah would arrive?

With all this in mind, we can now join the noisy crowds in Jerusalem for one very special Feast of Tabernacles, the one where Jesus took centre stage.

As we said before, it is estimated that about three-quarters of John's Gospel is directly related to events that occurred at the various feasts, so we ought to turn to that gospel now. Pause at this point to read John chapter 7, but don't stop there just because of the chapter division. Keep going through chapters 8 and 9, and even into chapter 10. This will pay dividends later.

John chapter 7 records a key moment in the life of Jesus. This is the one time we read of Jesus going to the Feast of Tabernacles. Presumably he had been there on previous occasions, but this is now just six months before his death.

The chapter opens by telling us that Jesus was deliberately keeping away from Jerusalem at this time, preferring to stay in Galilee due to the likelihood that the Jews in Judea would try to kill him. But once the time for the Feast of Tabernacles drew near his unbelieving brothers begin to taunt him. 'People are saying you're acting like the Messiah, so this is your big moment. Go to the feast. They're expecting a Messiah at this time, so go to the big city and show them what you can do' (see John 7:2-5). Behind this mockery is the implication that if you don't take this opportunity then clearly you don't think you are the Messiah. And if you do go, it might put an end to all this nonsense!

Jesus' reply is forceful but also a bit mysterious (John 7:6-9). We might read into it now that he knew it was not yet his time to die. This had to occur at Passover. Quite what his brothers made of his words isn't recorded, but with all this talk of 'the right time' they might have assumed that he was backing out from all the publicity for a year at least.

However, it seems Jesus always intended to go after all, but he waited until the feast had already begun, perhaps to avoid having to travel with his unbelieving brothers, but maybe also to avoid a public entrance which would attract too much attention too soon. Notice that in his absence many were already engaging in messianic speculation. Whispered rumours centred on whether he was genuine or a deceiver. Meanwhile, the Jewish leaders were keeping an eye out for him in the way that Jesus had anticipated (John 7:11-13).

When Jesus eventually arrives in Jerusalem three or four days have passed. The feast is already at its halfway point. Once there he does exactly what was expected of any well-known rabbi at one of the major feasts. He goes to the Temple courts and teaches. At festivals such as this, famous rabbis always 'set up shop', holding outdoor sessions for the benefit of visiting pilgrims who may not otherwise have much chance to hear them. Jesus joins in, with the inevitable outcome that people are amazed at his learning and in particular his authority. As a result, messianic expectation intensifies further (John 7:25-31). Is this really the one we are waiting for? Above all, people wanted to know what the authorities had concluded about this man. Their decision would be crucial in telling them what to believe.

Notice that part of the debate about whether Jesus was the Messiah focused on his place of birth. Some held to the idea quite common at the time that the Messiah's origins would be shrouded in mystery (John 7:27). His birthplace would be obscure and his parents unknown. This strange belief may have been based upon the mysterious Melchizedek who appeared to Abraham in Genesis 14:18-20 (see also Hebrews chapter 7, especially verse 3). Others knew their scriptures well enough to say that the Messiah would come from Bethlehem (John 7:42). But the problem was that everyone knew where Jesus had come from – Nazareth! And this was in the Galilee, no less! The fact that he was really a Bethlehem baby was not generally known. However, Jesus' main concern was not whether they knew his real birthplace, which he never revealed anyway, but whether or not they recognised his heavenly or divine origin (see John 7:28-29, 41-43).

Where things really get interesting is in John 7:37. We have now reached the last and greatest day of the feast, that's the seventh day or the Day of the Great Hosanna. We've already seen that on this day the celebration of the water offering comes to a climax with a magnificent procession to the Pool of Siloam to draw water, which would then be poured out before the altar in the Temple. Part of the reason for doing this was to thank God for the recent harvest but also to petition him for further rain, which was needed soon if they were to start sowing ready for the next harvest.

However, you may recall from the previous chapter that by the time of Jesus the water ceremony also had a prophetic or messianic aspect, especially regarding the outpouring of the Spirit of God upon all people. It is at this moment in the feast that Jesus dramatically draws attention to himself using this powerful element of the feast. He places himself right at the centre of it all and declares in a loud voice that this is really all about him. He alone can provide the living water, something he had previously said to a woman at a well in Samaria (John 4:9-15). He adds that the true fulfilment of the water offering is the outpouring of the Spirit which he will provide for those who believe in him, a promise he will make good later in the year at another one of the *moedim*, Pentecost. Overall, Jesus is speaking right into the heart of the symbolism of Tabernacles, boldly making claims about himself via something they already knew well. Imagine the impact his words would have had in those circumstances!

So what about the light aspect of the feast? Did he do the same with that? If you have already read on into chapter 8 you will see that he did, in verse 12, where he said, 'I am the light of the world. Whoever follows me will never walk in darkness but will have the light of life.' Let's see what happened leading up to this statement.

After all the debate and division over Jesus and the water ceremony, everyone goes home for a good night's rest. Jesus spends the night on the Mount of Olives. Fortunately, he hasn't been arrested by the Temple guards as the chief priests and Pharisees had hoped, and he's back in the Temple courts by dawn the next day.

Now anyone who just starts reading from the beginning of chapter 8 may not be aware which day this is. But following from chapter 7 we know this is still the Feast of Tabernacles and must now be the eighth day, or Simchat Torah. Some commentators have said that Jesus' declaration about living water actually took place on the eighth day when there was no water offering, that he waited until this was all over before making his claims. In which case John chapter 8 must now be on the next day after that, just after Tabernacles has concluded. But it is much more likely that John 7:37 is referring to the seventh day, the real last day and climax, and much more realistic for Jesus to take up the water symbolism when it was actually occurring. Moreover, the following eighth day is Simchat Torah, a celebration of the Law, and the Law is what John 8:1-11 is all about.

Notice that teachers of the Law are now involved (John 8:3), and verse 5 starts with 'In the Law Moses commanded ...' A case of adultery is brought before Jesus for him to make a ruling. Will he keep to the Mosaic Law or not? Jesus knows this is a trap. He probably suspects this is a set-up. They seem to have let the man go for a start and it would have been relatively easy during the night to have found such illicit goings-on among the thousands camped around Jerusalem.

Jesus' approach is interesting and significant. At first he says nothing. Instead he starts writing in the dust. Why? And what did he write? For a start, recall that this eighth day is a special Sabbath. All the usual Sabbath laws applied, including refraining from writing as this was regarded as work but only if it left a permanent mark such as ink on paper. Writing in the dust was therefore allowed. According to the Mishnah, a later collection of Jewish writings based on the oral law: 'If a man wrote with liquids or with fruit-juice or with dust from the roads or with writer's sand or with aught that leaves no lasting mark, he is not culpable' (Mishnah, Shabbat, 12:5). In this case, in John chapter 8, the wind or someone's feet would soon obliterate what Jesus had written, so he was acting fully in accordance with Sabbath rules. And we will never know what he actually wrote!

Some think he may have copied out the particular law which says she should be stoned to death (Lev. 20:10, Deut. 22:22). Incidentally, this law also states that the man must be put to death as well. Maybe Jesus was reminding them of this. But more likely, by writing on the stone floor of the Temple courts his action is reminiscent of the time when the commandments were written on tablets of stone by the finger of God. If so, Jesus is declaring that he knows the Law better than them. He was involved in writing it!

If Jesus *was* copying one of the laws, perhaps it was Deuteronomy 17:7 which says that the hands of the witnesses must be the first in putting someone to death. This was to dissuade people from making accusations they weren't prepared to follow through. This fits what Jesus says when he does eventually speak to them, only he adds that the first stone-thrower must be entirely guilt free. The situation has changed dramatically. His opponents are now faced with a test of their own, one they cannot pass. They look at each other but no-one will take up the challenge. Not even the eldest has the courage, so one by one they slink away.

In all this we see something we mentioned in one of our previous chapters (Chapter Twenty-Three) on the Law of Moses. Jesus said he had come to fulfil the Law, meaning he would interpret it properly, or in this case fairly. By dealing with the woman in this way, Jesus is not denying the original law, or annulling it, but saying the accusers did not follow the law properly themselves. They had let the man go (remember, she had been caught in the act of adultery, so the man must have been there). Nor did they have the moral right to execute the required punishment. In addition, legally, Jesus himself could not stone her as he hadn't witnessed her adultery, so she is free to go, admonished but still alive. And all this on Simchat Torah, the day of rejoicing over the Law. She can now go and join in the celebrations.

Meanwhile, this whole scene had taken place before a large crowd who had gathered round Jesus to hear him teach

(John 8:2). So teach them he does, by announcing that he is the light of the world (John 8:12). The four gigantic *menorah* were still lit, illuminating the whole Temple area where all this had happened. As the end of the feast was approaching they would soon be extinguished. But Jesus was still with them, the true light. If people followed him they needn't walk in darkness. What they had just witnessed needn't happen again, either the misdeeds of the woman or the schemes of her accusers.

There is a lot more still to occur on this final day of the Feast of Tabernacles, including the events of chapter 9 and on until John 10:21. After that we switch to another feast, the Feast of Dedication or Hanukkah, a few weeks later. This was not one of the biblical *moedim* but was part of the Jewish calendar at this time, and Jesus seems happy to have attended it.

But we can't end this chapter without mentioning a few points from John chapter 9 where again Jesus says, 'I am the light of the world' (John 9:5). In this case the light he is bringing is not about moral behaviour or a proper understanding of the law, but a physical healing, sight to the blind. In this chapter a man born blind will experience light for the first time, and as a result slowly come to realise that Jesus is indeed the Messiah. Jesus could have healed him in many ways, but he chose a strange method involving saliva and mud. Why? So that he could go and wash it all away. Where? At the Pool of Siloam of course! Where else at this time? Once again this provoked a lot of debate about who Jesus was, culminating in the divided opinions expressed in John 10:20-21.

These chapters in John's Gospel are all centred on this important feast, and what Jesus said and did there truly comes to life once we realise this.

There are two more things to say regarding Jesus and the Feast of Tabernacles, which we will leave to the next chapter, which is also the final one, when we will also sum up what this feast can mean for us today.

Chapter Twenty-Seven

Jesus and Us

In the last chapter we looked at John's Gospel, especially chapter 7, to see what happened when Jesus visited the Feast of Tabernacles just six months before his death. We said at the end of that chapter that before we sum up what this feast can mean for us today we still had a bit more to consider concerning Jesus and Tabernacles. Two things in particular require our attention: his birth and his return.

The full cycle of *moedim*, or God's appointed times, was designed with the Messiah in mind. Most people realise that Jesus fulfilled the Spring Feasts: Passover through his death, Firstfruits by his resurrection and Pentecost with the outpouring of the Spirit. But perhaps the reason why we know less about the Autumn Feasts, especially Tabernacles, is that we have yet to recognise how these feature within the life of Jesus. If Jesus did everything according to God's timetable as enshrined within the biblical calendar then perhaps he fulfilled these too, especially as Tabernacles became the time that the Messiah was expected to appear? It would certainly create a neat cycle if he was born and destined to return in accordance with this feast. So could his first appearance on earth and his second really be in fulfilment of the Feast of Tabernacles? Let's review the evidence.

It's now well known that Jesus wasn't actually born on the twenty-fifth of December. This date for celebrating the birth of Jesus began in Rome in the fourth century, chosen as it coincided with the winter solstice, a pagan midwinter festival. The idea was that by incorporating this into Christianity it would somehow be 'Christianised' and its pagan influence lessened. It also had the advantage of fitting in with the idea, albeit totally unsubstantiated, that the conception of Jesus took place in the spring, in particular on the twenty-fifth of March.

You will notice that all this is based upon our Roman calendar rather than the biblical one. Other attempts to move Jesus' birth away from December are also similarly based upon our culture and climate. For example, Jesus cannot have been born in the winter as there were sheep in the fields, so springtime is more likely. But what about the autumn, especially around Tabernacles in late September, early October? There would be shepherds in the field in the Middle East at this time, but is there any biblical proof to support this theory? With careful reading and a bit of detective work, evidence does emerge.

In Luke chapter 1 we learn that the birth of John the Baptist was foretold by the angel Gabriel, and six months later this same angel visited Mary with similar news. Gabriel announced the birth of John to his father, Zechariah, a priest, while he was serving in the Temple, burning incense at the altar. We can assume John the Baptist was conceived very soon after this, if not that same night, especially as Zechariah's lack of belief in Gabriel's message meant he was to remain dumb until his son was born, an incentive not to wait too long.

If Jesus was conceived shortly after Gabriel's visit to Mary, six months later, and born nine months after this, then we have a total of fifteen months from Zechariah's experience in the Temple to the birth of Jesus. Even allowing for a bit of flexibility this gives a good idea of when Jesus was born provided we know at what time of the year Zechariah entered the Temple to burn incense. And we can deduce this from Luke chapter 1 together with one of those passages in the Old Testament which we tend to ignore as not being that interesting.

Luke tells us that Zechariah was of the priestly division of Abijah and was chosen by lot from that division to serve in the Temple at that time (Luke 1:5-10). Each of the priestly divisions had a specific time of year when they were on duty in the Temple, fixed according to a rota which can be found in 1 Chronicles chapter 24. There, in verse 10, we learn that Abijah was eighth out of the twenty-four divisions, putting it a third of the way through the year, so within the fourth month. Add on the fifteen months we calculated above and we get to the seventh month of the following year, that month being Tishrei, the month of the Feast of Tabernacles. Is this enough to convince us that Jesus was born at this time?

If not we could also consider the way John describes the birth of Jesus in the opening chapter of his gospel. It is well known that John records that 'The Word [*logos*] became flesh and made his dwelling among us' (John 1:14). In the second part of this sentence, 'made his dwelling' is a Greek word, *eskenosen*, based upon *skene* which means 'tabernacle' or 'tent'. Literally, John is saying that by taking on a body like ours the *Logos* pitched his tent or 'tabernacled' among us. The Word becoming flesh can be compared to someone putting up a tent or temporary shelter as he came to stay on earth for a while.

Did John know something we don't about when Jesus was born? Did this influence how John described Jesus coming to dwell amongst men? Perhaps. It could of course be argued that this symbolism is still appropriate whatever time of year it occurred. Or it might be another clue for our detective work, especially if we believe that Tabernacles was fulfilled by the Messiah in some way.

So if his birth starts the cycle of *moedim*, could it be that his return completes it, back where it started, also at Tabernacles? Bear in mind that what for us will be his second appearance on earth will effectively be his first for Jews who have yet to acknowledge Jesus as their Messiah. For them, they are still awaiting their Messiah and expect him to come at this time of Tabernacles.

The main objection to saying that Jesus will return at this feast comes from something Jesus himself said, namely that no-one knows, or can know, the day or hour of his return. Jesus made this clear in his teaching towards the end of the Gospels (Mark 13:32; Matthew 24:36, 25:13). So suggesting he will return at the Feast of Tabernacles seems to contradict this and be tantamount to date fixing which is regarded as a big error, even false teaching or false prophecy.

This phrase of Jesus has always been intriguing especially as he also gives many signs as to his return. How can we not know if we have so many signposts or signals to prepare us? Unbelievers will naturally ignore these or be ignorant of them, so they won't know anything about when he might return. They are not expecting it at all, even scoffing at the possibility. But disciples of Jesus should be more aware and so be alert as the time approaches. It could also be argued that the Feast of Tabernacles is not just a single day anyway. It stretches over eight days so it is still possible not to know the actual day or hour as it could be anytime during this week. But even pinpointing any particular week of the year can still seem to contradict what Jesus said and so alarms some people.

However, all this misses the real impact of what Jesus said. His words can be taken purely at face value to mean no-one can know anything at all about when he will return. But then why does he specifically say 'no-one knows the day or hour' when it would be enough to just say 'day' or just say 'hour'. Why both?

The reason is because this phrase was a Jewish expression or idiom specifically used in connection with one of the *moedim*, namely the Feast of Trumpets, the day when these Autumn Feasts begin. The Feast of Trumpets was known as 'the feast that no-one knows the day or hour of'. Why was this? You can look up the details online if you want to know more, but here is the short version.

The Jewish calendar at the time of Jesus was based upon the moon which by God's design marked the months of the year (Gen. 1:14). Every month started with a new moon. There was no exact calendar date fixed in advance. Instead, a month began by observation of the moon. The Sanhedrin or Jewish ruling council in Jerusalem had to declare the official start of each month. This was done according to the testimony of at least two reliable witnesses who had seen the new moon appear and reported this to the Sanhedrin. It may be known roughly when this should happen, but everyone had to wait for official confirmation. No-one could know in advance exactly which day this would be. But once the month had officially begun you could count ahead and determine accurately when feasts such as Passover or Pentecost should take place.

However, the Feast of Trumpets was unique in that it was the only one of the *moedim* due to take place on the *first* day of a month (Tishrei). That's why it was the only feast of which it could be said 'no-one knows the day or hour'. You knew it was coming but not exactly when. You just had to be ready and waiting.

The Jewish context is always fascinating and illuminating, and clearly Jesus was drawing on this as an illustration of his return. But through his 'no-one knows' statement was he cryptically giving us the date after all, though not the year? It may be tempting to conclude this, even now that the Jewish calendar is fixed, but for many this would still be taking things too far. However, even if the day of his return does not coincide with the Feast of Trumpets, it is still valid and relevant to compare aspects of his return with the Autumn feasts. His return will be heralded by the sound of trumpets, and followed by a time of harvest, an ingathering of God's people, including Gentiles. We saw in an earlier chapter that the Feast of Tabernacles had a harvest element, and also through the seventy bulls sacrificed, it looked ahead to Gentiles being included in God's kingdom. In addition, Tabernacles was a time of great thanksgiving and joy. Surely this will also be the case when Jesus returns?

The *moedim* were tied to the annual agricultural cycle of the land but also represented God's plan for the ages. Jesus was to be the suffering Messiah of the Spring Feasts, and the returning King of the Autumn Feasts, at which time a new year or age will begin, the messianic age or millennial reign. If we believe he fulfilled the first cluster, why not also the second?

There is one other intriguing feature to consider. On the second day of Succoth the traditional reading from the prophets is Zechariah chapter 14. In verses 16-19 of that chapter we find that the Feast of Tabernacles will still be celebrated once Jesus has returned. It will be part of his messianic kingdom. Indeed it seems to be the only one of the *moedim* still in effect. All nations, which therefore includes Gentiles, will come to Jerusalem for this feast. We may not be sure exactly what this will involve but it shows that Tabernacles somehow transcends our present world and experience. It belongs to our future in some way. Our future with Jesus.

Even if the actual dates of Jesus' birth and return remain uncertain, there is still much to learn from Succoth and the associated period. Some may find that Tabernacles provides a quieter, more appropriate, time of year to reflect on the birth of Jesus and its true meaning, away from the traditional Christmas with all its commercialism and consumerism. Equally, we could benefit from a regular time when we focus on Christ's return and what will follow, something which is lacking in our current calendar. The Autumn Feasts can rectify this. In particular, thinking of Jesus' return at the Feast of Trumpets and then of his birth at Tabernacles, starting the cycle again, could put the rest of the year into a better perspective.

Succoth also makes us aware of an aspect of our salvation we often overlook. It reminds us this is a journey from the day of our conversion to the day of our final salvation when Jesus returns, a journey which often takes place through a wilderness where our only security is to be found in God himself.

Succoth involves making ourselves vulnerable for a while. We put ourselves into a flimsy and fragile place in order to let go of all we regard as substantial, so that what is unseen becomes more real. This is not a total renunciation of such things, just a reflection on their limitations and that occasionally we need time apart from them. If we are willing to go into our *sukkah* for a while we can find tremendous release and blessing. We realise that much of what we hold on to in life is actually holding on to us and, as Ecclesiastes declares, is ultimately empty, even meaningless. But Ecclesiastes also teaches that we can rediscover the value and enjoyment of life in this world if we see it as a gift from God.

We love the liberty of Passover and desire the power of Pentecost, but we also need Succoth to remind us that this life is transient. We are merely passing through, but with a future thanks to the one who tabernacled on earth for us. Moreover, the only future we can have is with him. It is his future that we will be sharing.

We commented in an earlier chapter how the Jews called Tabernacles 'the season of our joy', a time when rejoicing was to the full and to the fore. We could learn much from this. There are many texts in the New Testament which command us to be joyful or to rejoice in the Lord but how often do we do this? Tabernacles challenges us in this area also.

Let's end by recalling in Nehemiah 8:17 that when they rediscovered this feast in the Word of God, they immediately put it into practice with the result that 'their joy was very great'.

Listening to the Jewish Jesus

ISBN: 978-1-915046-65-9

Paul Luckraft's new book explores the Hebraic nature of the teaching of Jesus and shows how a first-century rabbi spoke to other Jews of the time and in particular taught his disciples. What can we expect to find from such an exploration, and what can this mean for us today?

Jesus used many Hebraic idioms, expressions commonly used in one language but which make less sense in another. Someone outside the culture or who is not a native speaker can easily be confused. A better grasp of such Hebraisms within the gospels will greatly improve our understanding of what Jesus is saying to us.

In his teaching Jesus often hinted at the Jewish scriptures, employing the rabbinic technique of *remez*. These allusions to the Old Testament would be readily picked up by his listeners but we can miss them. We need to find these and unpack the depths of their meaning.

Jesus' teaching also reflects aspects of first-century Judaism with which we are largely unfamiliar and need to appreciate more fully. One of these is the relationship between a rabbi and his disciples, a theme which occupies the first part of the book.

This book will help those who teach the Bible as well as provide a companion for anyone wanting to read the gospels more accurately and follow Jesus more closely.

Come and listen afresh to the Jewish Jesus.